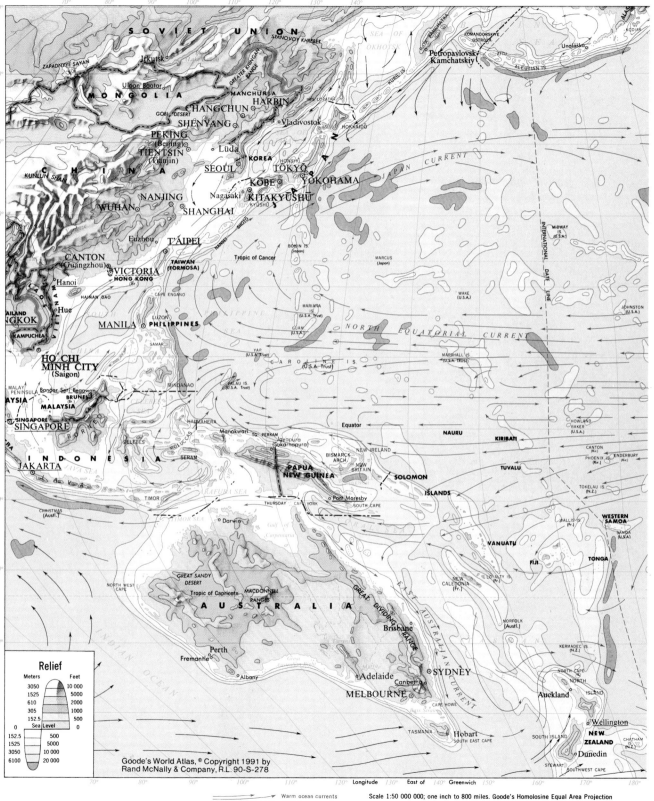

Relief

Meters	Feet
3050	10 000
1525	5000
610	2000
305	1000
152.5	500
0 Sea Level	0
152.5	500
1525	5000
3050	10 000
6100	20 000

Warm ocean currents
Cold ocean currents

Scale 1:50 000 000; one inch to 800 miles. Goode's Homolosine Equal Area Projection
Elevations and depressions are given in feet

Longitude East of Greenwich

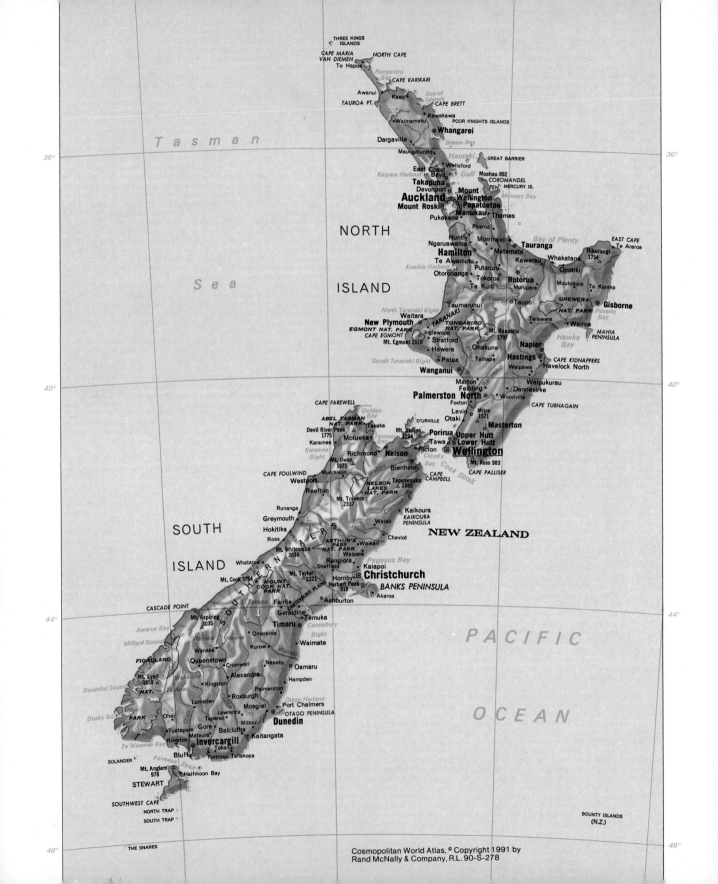

THREE KINGS
ISLANDS

CAPE MARIA
VAN DIEMEN   NORTH CAPE
Te Hapua
Rangaunu
Bay   CAPE KARIKARI

Awanui   Kaeo   *Bay of*
TAUROA PT.   *Islands* CAPE BRETT
Kawakawa
Waimamaku   POOR KNIGHTS ISLANDS
Whangarei
Dargaville   *Bream Bay*

Maungaturoto   *Hauraki*   GREAT BARRIER

T a s m a n   *Kaipara Harbour* Wellsford   *Gulf*   Moehau 892   GREAT BARRIER IS.
East Coast Bays   COROMANDEL
Takapuna   PEN. MERCURY IS.
Devonport   **Mount**   *Mercury Bay*
Auckland Wellington
Mount Roskill **Papatoetoe**
Manukau Thames
Pukekohe

Paeroa   *Bay of Plenty*   EAST CAPE
NORTH   Huntly   Te Araroa
Ngaruawahia Morrinsville   **Tauranga**   Hikurangi
Hamilton Matamata Kawerau Whakatane   1754
S e a   Te Awamutu   Putaruru   Opotiki
ISLAND   *Kawhia Harbour* Otorohanga Tokoroa **Rotorua** Moutohora Te Kaha
Te Kuiti   Murupara   UREWERA
Taupo   NAT. PARK **Gisborne**
North Taranaki Bight Taumarunui   Taupo   *Poverty*
Waitara   TARANAKI Tarawera   *Bay*
New Plymouth NAT. PARK   Wairoa
EGMONT NAT. PARK Inglewood Mt. Ruapehu   Napier   MAHIA
CAPE EGMONT Stratford   2797   PENINSULA
Mt. Egmont 2518 Hawera Ohakune   **Napier**
South Taranaki Bight Patea Taihape **Hastings** CAPE KIDNAPPERS
Waipawa   Havelock North

Wanganui   *Hawke*
Marton   *Bay*
Feilding Waipukurau
40°   CAPE FAREWELL   **Palmerston North** Dannevirke   40°
Foxton   Woodville
Golden   Levin Mitre CAPE TURNAGAIN
ABEL TASMAN   *Bay* Otaki   1571
NAT. PARK Takaka   D'URVILLE   **Masterton**
Devil River Peak Mt. Stokes **Porirua** Upper Hutt
1775   Motueka 1204   Tawa   Lower Hutt
Karamea   *Tasman* Picton **Wellington**
Karamea   Richmond *Bay* **Nelson**   Mt. Ross 983
Bight Mt. Owen   Blenheim   *Cloudy*
1875   Murchison   *Bay.* *Cook*   CAPE PALLISER
CAPE FOULWIND   NELSON Tapusenuku CAPE   *Strait*
Westport LAKES 2885 CAMPBELL
Reefton NAT. PARK
Mt. Travers
SOUTH   2337
Runanga   Kaikoura
Greymouth   KAIKOURA
Hokitika   Waiau   PENINSULA   NEW ZEALAND
ISLAND   Ross   Cheviot
ARTHUR'S Waikari
Mt. Whitcombe PASS
Whataroa   2638 NAT. PARK Waipara
Rangiora
Sheffield Kaiapoi *Pegasus Bay*
Mt. Taylor
Mt. Cook 3764   2321 Hornby **Christchurch**
MOUNT   Herbert Peak BANKS PENINSULA
COOK NAT.   918
PARK   Ashburton Akaroa
CASCADE POINT   Fairlie
Geraldine *Canterbury*
Mt. Aspiring Temuka   *Bight*
3035   **Timaru**
Awarua Bay Omarama   *Canterbury*
Milford Sound Kurow *Plains*
Waimate
FIORDLAND Wanaka *Hawea*
Mt. Lyall Cromwell Oamaru
Doubtful Sound 1859 Queenstown Naseby
Alexandra Hampden
Kingston
Dusky Sd. Lumsden   Roxburgh Palmerston
NAT. Mosgiel Port Chalmers
Ohai   Lawrence Milton OTAGO PENINSULA
Te Waewae Bay PARK Tuatapere Mataura **Dunedin**
Gore Balclutha
SOLANDER Riverton Kaitangata
Mt. Anglem **Invercargill** Tokanui
978   Bluff Fortrose Tahakopa
STEWART Halfmoon Bay

SOUTHWEST CAPE
NORTH TRAP   BOUNTY ISLANDS
SOUTH TRAP   (N.Z.)

THE SNARES

PACIFIC

OCEAN

Cosmopolitan World Atlas, © Copyright 1991 by
Rand McNally & Company, R.L. 90-S-278

Enchantment of the World

NEW ZEALAND

By Mary Virginia Fox

Consultant for New Zealand: S.F. Newman, B.A. [N.Z.], M.A. (Auck), Dip. Tchng [N.Z.], Principal Lecturer in Social Sciences, Christchurch Teachers' College, Christchurch, New Zealand

Consultant for Reading: Robert L. Hillerich, Ph.D., Visiting Professor, University of South Florida; Consultant, Pinellas County Schools, Florida

CHILDRENS PRESS®

CHICAGO

Maori women performing a traditional dance

Library of Congress Cataloging-in-Publication Data

Fox, Mary Virginia.
    New Zealand / by Mary Virginia Fox.
        p.   cm. — (Enchantment of the world)
    Includes index.
    Summary: Introduces New Zealand, first populated by
the Maori, who named the land mass "Land of the Long
White Cloud."
    ISBN 0-516-02728-X
    1. New Zealand—Juvenile literature. 2. New
Zealand. I. Title. II. Series.
DU408.F68   1991   90-20010
993—dc20   CIP
                                                           AC

Picture Acknowledgments
AP/Wide World Photos: 48
The Bettmann Archive: 19, 20 (right)
© **Cameramann International, Ltd.:** 67 (right), 79 (right),
89 (top left), 95 (top left), 115 (left)
© **Virginia R. Grimes:** 115 (right)
H. Armstrong Roberts: © E. R. Degginger, 50;
© **C. Bryant,** 61, 65; © **Zefa,** 91
Historical Pictures Service, Chicago: 26, 27 (2 photos), 31
(2 photos), 33, 35, 36 (2 photos)
Journalism Services: © Dave Brown, 6 (left)
Kirkendall/Spring: 8, 79 (left)
© **Emilie Lepthien:** 38 (bottom), 62
North Wind Picture Archives: 28, 38 (top)

Odyssey/Frerck/Chicago: © **Robert Frerck,** 10 (left), 12
(bottom), 18, 64 (bottom), 67 (left), 68, 76 (bottom), 81
(2 photos), 82 (bottom left), 93 (left), 95 (top & bottom
right), 105 (right), 114
Peabody Museum of Salem: 15, 20 (left), 22, 23
Photri: 16, 53, 54 (left), 55, 57 (bottom left), 63, 69 (left),
88, 101; © **J. Allan Cash Ltd.,** 54 (right)
© **Pivan/Morrison:** 57 (bottom right)
© **Porterfield/Chickering:** 4, 17 (right), 75, 77 (right), 82
(bottom right), 85, 87, 102
Root Resources: © **Russel A. Kriete,** 5, 93 (right)
© **James P. Rowan:** 72, 77 (left), 108
Tom Stack & Associates: © **Dave Watts,** 10 (right); © **John
Cancalosi,** 11 (top left), 82 (top right); © **Manfred
Gottschalk,** 21 (right); © **C. Benjamin,** 74; © **Kevin
Schaffer,** 116
SuperStock International, Inc.: 52 (left), 71, 76 (top);
© **Warren Jacobs,** Cover, 6 (top & bottom right), 40 (right),
64 (top), 78, 105 (left), 107; © **John Spooner,** 9; © **W.
Burkhart,** 12 (top); © **Howard Hughes,** 17 (left); © **Robin
Smith,** 21 (left), 89 (bottom), 111; © **Ray Manley,** 24;
© **Manley Features,** 58; © **Ann & Myron Sutton,** 73
TSW-CLICK/Chicago: 117 (2 photos); © **Dallas & John
Heaton,** 40 (left), 60, 66; © **Kim Christensen,** 56; © **Roger
Wood,** 59; © **Ronald Gordon,** 69 (right), 70; © **Karen
Phillips,** 98
Valan: © **Kennon Cooke,** Cover Inset, 13, 52 (right), 57
(top), 80, 95 (bottom left), 99; © **Tom W. Parkin,** 11
(bottom left); © **Arthur Christiansen,** 11 (right)
Len W. Meents: Maps on 51, 55, 58, 67, 70, 74, 76, 80
**Courtesy Flag Research Center, Winchester,
Massachusetts 01890:** Flag on back cover
Cover: Shotover River, Queenstown, New Zealand
Cover Inset: Maori totems, Government Gardens,
Rotorua, New Zealand

Hiking on Franz Josef Glacier in Westland National Park

TABLE OF CONTENTS

The varied landscape of
New Zealand: Nikau palms
along the west coast
of South Island (top right),
spectacular waterfalls in
Milford Sound (above),
and fertile rolling land (right)

Chapter 1

SHAPING THE LAND

New Zealand is a land thrust up out of the ocean by the violent action of volcanoes. She is surrounded on all sides by a vast underwater seascape of ridges and trenches, as if a giant crumpled ball of paper had been thrown on the floor of the world, then covered by water. Submarine volcanoes are continually shaping contours. As the land is thrust upward, it is being worn away by rivers and coastlines are being nibbled away by the sea.

Today it is a land of majestic snowcapped mountains, nearly impenetrable rain forests, rolling meadows, crystal lakes, tumbling waterfalls, boiling geysers, and fiords that cut inland in deep fingers of water. It is a beautiful, spectacular country—a kaleidoscope of contrasts.

New Zealand's two main islands are appropriately named North Island and South Island. There are other small rocky bits of land that jut out of the water. Some are large enough for permanent settlements. Others are uninhabited.

These unusual rock formations at Punakaiki are called the Pancake Rocks.

New Zealand also serves as a protectorate government for the Cook Islands, the nearby island of Niue, the three islands of the Tokelau chain, and the vast area of the Antarctic called the Ross Dependency.

New Zealand has not always been a country of islands. In prehistoric times it was once a part of New Caledonia, Australia, Tasmania, and Antarctica. Huge continental plates, large sections of the outer crust of the earth, slowly drifted apart. About fifty-five million years ago, Australia and New Zealand began their long journey northward into warmer seas as Antarctica headed

*White Island, in the Bay of Plenty, has an active
volcano that is constantly emitting clouds of smoke.*

south to become locked in ice. The results of the violent
wrenching of the earth are seen today in the geological *faults*,
splits in the rock, that crisscross New Zealand.

As the earth masses parted, the sea moved in. The Antarctic
Circumpolar Current, the world's largest, was created, circulating
clockwise around the entire Antarctic continent. This gave rise to
the system of prevailing westerly winds, at latitudes between 40 to
60 degrees south, that had much to do with the settlement of New
Zealand. Sailors have long named them the Roaring Forties,
Furious Fifties, and Screaming Sixties because of the intense and
constant power they create.

The flightless kiwi (left) and a soaring albatross (right)

ANIMALS AND PLANTS

The newly formed oceans blocked the passage of migrating forms of life. The only mammals in New Zealand's early existence were a type of primitive bat who were able to cross water before the ocean became too wide and stormy. The ancestors of some of New Zealand's distinctive native birds probably arrived at the same time.

The islands' birds include dozens of varieties found only in New Zealand, for example, the flightless kiwi, whose name New Zealanders have adopted as their nickname. Colorful parrots abound in some of the northern areas, and there is the noisy kaka, which grows fat on native berries. There also are lovely songbirds native to the country, the most beautiful sounds perhaps coming from the bellbird. The albatross, oystercatcher, and other seabirds found their way here, too.

*A herd of red deer (left),
a tuatara (top left),
and a hedgehog (above)*

But the open water kept some unwanted visitors from the land. New Zealand shares its record of being snake-free with only two other island countries in the world—Ireland and New Caledonia. Only one reptile has been found here, a completely harmless but frightening-looking lizard, called a tuatara, which belongs to the age of the dinosaur.

Most of New Zealand's animals did not originate here but were imported by various settler groups. The Maori brought dogs and rats, both used as food. Captain Cook released some pigs, whose wild descendants are still about. Other imports include the red deer, opossum, hedgehog, weasel, and rabbit, which was brought in for its pelt and meat.

11

Ferns (above) sometimes grow
as tall as trees. The Maori
used the kauri pine (left)
for their seagoing canoes.
Now the kauri are
protected and harvests
are controlled.

Resin, or "gum," from the kauri pine

Particularly in the South Island, lush forests cover the lower shoulders of the mountains. The forests of New Zealand are called "the bush," but they differ widely from one geographical area to another. In the northern warmer regions there is a luxurious growth of ferns, some growing as tall as trees. The stately kauri trees, whose hardwood trunks are unblemished by knots and other imperfections, were prized for building ships and houses by the early settlers.

The kauri pines left another form of treasure. The sap from the trees left a sticky gum that in time hardened and was buried in leaf mold and soil. Modern man found a use for the strange lumps that were often the size of a human head. "Gum diggers" sold their finds at high prices to chemical companies that used them in the manufacture of lacquers and varnishes.

During December and January, North Island cliffs and lakeshores are a mass of scarlet when the pohutukawa (or Christmas tree) bursts into bloom, while the rata is doing likewise in the South Island. New Zealand has an astounding array of flowering plants, a full 80 percent of which are not found anywhere else in the world. The undisputed queen of blossoms has to be the world's largest buttercup. There are sixty varieties of daisies and a curious plant called the "vegetable sheep," which looks like sheep in a close-up view.

DISCOVERING *AOTEAROA*

New Zealand was first populated by the Maori, who were Polynesians. Polynesian is a rather general term that includes several distinctive groups of common origin that inhabited the Pacific Islands. The Maori are just one of these groups. The Maori are a people entirely distinct from the Australian aborigines who have been living in their homeland for more than twenty-five thousand years.

In remote history the Maori people probably lived somewhere near what we now call India. They eventually worked their way east to what is now Indonesia. When pressure from other ethnic groups sent them searching for a land they could call their own, they turned to the sea.

Two inventions made it possible for the Maori to travel across the ocean. One was the sail, but this left a canoe vulnerable to being overturned when the wind was strong. So these early sailors developed the outrigger, a poled extension on at least one side of their craft, which stabilized the boat.

Centuries ago Polynesians spread out over the Pacific, colonizing specks of land wherever they could provide food and shelter for their families. The Maori lived on an island they called *Hawaiki*. It was somewhere in the north Pacific, but we do not know just where.

Sometime between the years A.D. 800 and 1350 (experts disagree on the exact date), a group of Maori again began searching for a homeland. According to legend based on fact, they set out in seven canoes ranging in size from forty to sixty feet (twelve to eighteen meters). Each canoe probably carried a chief and his *wahine* (wives) and about fifty followers. The only food these

In 1942, these Maori men, in a traditional canoe, welcomed the arrival of the U.S. 169th Infantry, 43rd Division, to Auckland.

explorers carried with them was dried fruit, dogs, rats, seeds, and some root vegetables they intended to plant in a new land. They had to depend on fish and birds they caught as they sailed and rainwater collected in gourds.

The canoes were named *Tainui, Te Arawa, Matanantua, Horouta, Tokomaru, Aotea,* and *Takitimu,* all names that have been repeated from one generation to another, indelibly adding to New Zealand's oral history. The seven groups tried to stay close together in their voyage through uncharted waters, but it is said that shortly before sighting land, they were scattered during a tremendous storm. Each group made landfall in a different part of the east coast of the North Island of New Zealand. Here they hauled their canoes ashore and set about building shelters.

These remarkable journeys were made in open boats, unprotected from sun or storm, long before Columbus sailed across the Atlantic equipped with compass and a Western education that gave him a knowledge of astronomy and navigation.

The area around Lake Pukaki does not look the same today as it did when the first Maori arrived.

What the Maori had discovered was a landmass much larger than Polynesians had encountered anywhere else in the Pacific. They called it *Aotearoa*, which in their tongue means "Land of the Long White Cloud." New Zealand's two islands stretch in a curve from north to south. Mountains jut high into the sky, some capped with fields of snow.

A reconstructed Maori village
(above) and a tiki (right)

ADAPTING TO THE NEW LAND

The Maori had to find new ways to build homes to protect them from the weather, which was colder than weather in Polynesia. For the first time lumber was available. They learned to use heavy wooden beams and posts to build their fortifications, storehouses, and dwellings. (Their meetinghouses, copies of missionary schoolhouses, probably were not built until the late eighteenth century after the Maori had had contact with Europeans.) They developed a complex and beautiful type of carving. Abstract scrolls and linear designs intertwined around stylized human figures, called *tiki*, that were a ritual symbol of fertility and protection. The faces had strange slanting eyes, often inlaid with iridescent paua (abalone) shells. Tongues were outstretched in a frightening sign of defiance.

The fertile Canterbury Plains

The Maori now depended on agriculture as well as the sea for food. The only produce they had harvested from the land of their ancestral home were coconuts, breadfruit, and bananas. These did not grow well in New Zealand, so they turned to other crops. They cleared the land by cutting trees and burning brush. They planted the roots of taro and kumara, a kind of potatolike yam. Here they found an ample supply of fern root, which soon became a delicacy, and they dug into the ground to collect a white slimy kind of grub they found delicious.

When they first arrived the Maori discovered a fine source of food in the moa, a spectacular flightless bird that stood 12-feet (3.6-meters) tall, twice as large as the ostrich found in Australia and South Africa today. The Maori became such skilled hunters that they killed the species to extinction. Their method of hunting was to burn the bush to drive the moa out. Repeated burning of the bush made the grasslands of the Canterbury Plains. Today bones and fossilized eggs of the giant creatures can be seen.

Maori women have always braided flax to be used for making baskets. Two women on the left are wearing capes made with bleached flax and black-dyed fiber.

The Maori also hunted whales, dolphins, and seal. Large ocean fish and shellfish were part of their diet. Human flesh was eaten "when procurable," which was one reason the Maori frequently waged war.

They harvested native flax, which was woven into fiber garments. For ceremonial occasions, fringed skirts were worn by both men and women. Striped cloaks of fiber, feathers, and dog skins were reserved for the chiefs. Flax also was used for rope and basket making. Rope was used to lash buildings together, since there were no nails.

The Maori had no metal to work with, but the new land provided stone materials for adzes, chisels, and drill points. They used varieties of bone for fishhooks and spearheads. Ornaments were carved from the supply of green stone, a form of jade, which was found principally on the west coast of the South Island.

A tattooed Maori woman (left) and a chief wearing a feather cape (right)

The Maori were a fierce-looking people, generally tall, with strong bodies. Their hair was slightly wavy. Their skin was light brown, frequently tattooed in intricate curving ridges. Men were usually marked on the face and buttocks. Some had their whole bodies decorated. Women were tattooed on the face and breasts.

The Maori's appearance lived up to their reputation as fearless warriors. Going into battle, they scared their enemies with blood-curdling screams, tongues out thrust, and war clubs waving. Today some of their ritual dances mimic this old tradition. New Zealand rugby football teams traditionally challenge their opponents with a dance called a *haka*.

When the Maori first arrived, they found the offshore islands inhabited by a smaller brown-skinned people they called the Moriori. The Maori quickly laid claim to the land by waging war. They eliminated their enemies by killing and eating them or by

Maori men perform the haka, *a dance intended to challenge opponents. The out-thrust tongue and bulging eyes were intended to scare enemies.*

intermarrying with the women of the race they came to dominate.

The last Moriori on the Chatham Islands, believed to be pure-blooded descendants of this original tribe, died in the twentieth century, wiped out by tuberculosis brought by later immigrants.

Waging war was not only a way to establish power over others. For individual males, as well as for tribes, it was a means to gain honor and prestige. The total count of enemy victims was kept in detail. The concept of *mana* (prestige) was an important way of life.

Conflicts between tribes were sometimes brought on by food shortages, but more often by a necessity to exert tribal power over territorial rights. Rarely were battles large or long lasting. They occurred usually in summer months, when the Maori were not engaged in farming or hunting. Often only a small raiding party was involved. There were few casualties, but being taken prisoner

A Maori settlement

was considered shameful to the defeated tribe and usually meant
death for the one captured and a good dinner for the captors.
Feuds frequently went on from generation to generation, as
gaining mana depended on taking *utu* (revenge) on the enemies of
one's kin.

The bulk of the population lived on North Island, particularly
on the coasts, where forests and the sea provided for most of their
needs. The Maori lived in a tribal society. Status was based on
ancestry, chieftains being able to trace links with leaders of the
past or back to the captains of the great canoes. Individual and
family possessions were few. Most items, in particular land, were
owned by the tribe.

Tribes were divided into groups called *hapus*. Settlements
ranging from a handful of households to more than five hundred
were frequently built on a hill for defense. Sometimes the
settlements were heavily fortified and they were referred to as a
pa. These were usually protected with a palisade of heavy timber
and ditches with sharp-pointed spikes. The Maori were skillful
engineers.

Maori natives of Te Taupan and Kotorua

Before the white man came, the weapons used were the *taiaha*, a long wooden-bladed knife, and short clubs, known as *patu* and *mere*. The Maori also were skilled in bringing down birds with the throwing stick, which came in two sizes—the heavy hunting variety and the graceful smaller ones.

Those who did not take part in battles were able to achieve recognition by their skill in building and crafts. With huge stands of tall trees to work with, war canoes became bigger and more elegant. They were not used anymore for long-distance exploration, but for coastal travel.

Priests and craftsmen, called *tohungas*, were high on the social scale. Tribal prestige depended on their leaders, and the prestige of the leaders was reflected in the ornateness of their appearance. Persons dressed according to their rank. The highest class was composed of hereditary nobles, *ariki*, and the military chiefs, *rangatira*. The commoners were the *tutua*. Slaves, who were lucky enough to be kept alive, did most of the menial work.

It was a highly developed culture Europeans found when they discovered the land.

The rugged peaks of the Southern Alps

Chapter 2

OTHERS DISCOVER THE LAND

DUTCH EXPLORERS

The southern Pacific was the last habitable part of the world to be reached by Europeans. Distances between islands, where ships could be provisioned, were not as great farther to the north, closer to the equator. But New Zealand was tucked down near the bottom of the globe, away from the normal routes of explorers and traders who had found and colonized parts of Asia, Africa, and North and South America.

Toward the end of the sixteenth century, the Dutch emerged as the greatest seafaring and trading nation of the western and central Pacific. They set up headquarters at Batavia, now known as Djakarta on the island of Java, and began searching for new trading partners and commodities.

New Zealand's two islands stretch some 1,000 miles (1,609 kilometers) from north to south. The mountains jut high into the sky, some capped with snow. A Dutch sea captain, Abel Janszoon Tasman, was the first white man to see New Zealand. On December 13, 1642, he saw what he described as "land uplifted high." He had sighted the Southern Alps of South Island. Despite

Abel Janszoon Tasman was the first white man to see New Zealand.

strong and heavy seas, he sailed northward up the coast and dropped anchor in a harbor now called Golden Bay. Tasman's first encounter with the Maori was not a friendly one. A canoe rammed a small boat dispatched from the captain's ship and fighting broke out. There was loss of life on both sides.

Tasman thought he had discovered a continent that ran across the Pacific to connect with the southern tip of South America, but he left before exploring the land, heading farther north to the Fiji group of islands.

Within a year other navigators discovered that the land Tasman had first sighted was two separate islands. They changed the name Tasman had given to the coast from *Statel 'andt* (the Dutch name for South America) to *Nieuw Zeeland* (New Zealand), but still no attempt was made to settle there.

It was 1769 before anyone bothered to find out what treasures the land held and who lived there. Captain James Cook, an

Captain James Cook (left) sailed his ship, the Endeavour, *(right), into Mercury Bay and claimed New Zealand for Great Britain.*

Englishman who was conducting a scientific expedition, sailed along the east coast of New Zealand. He saw many smoke fires ashore, suggesting there must be a large settlement of natives. The captain and a small landing party went ashore to investigate. Again there was violence when a band of Maori attacked four seamen left to guard the ship's boat.

Captain Cook had brought along a Tahitian chief as an interpreter, but the Maori were in no mood to talk. Cook and his men were forced to use muskets to get back to their ship at anchor. Three natives were killed.

Cook's ship, the *Endeavour*, sailed south into a bay that Cook called Mercury Bay after the planet that the ship's scientists had been observing. For the first time the explorers were able to make friends with the Maori. They traded trinkets for supplies of fish, birds, and water. It was here that Cook formally declared possession of the land in the name of the British crown.

South Sea whalers

Cook stayed in the area long enough to make accurate charts of the coastline. He then left for home at the end of March 1770, sailing up the eastern coast of Australia, past the Cape of Good Hope, to complete his round-the-world voyage. On two other occasions he returned for further exploration.

THE FIRST WHITE COLONIES

Within the next ten years, explorers covered the entire Pacific Ocean. What is now Sydney, Australia, was established as a British convict settlement, but still New Zealand was bypassed. For a while seal hunting along the southwest coast of the South Island brought large sailing ships to the harbors, but as the seals were killed off, the hunters moved on.

Next came the whalers at the turn of the century. None of these sailors went ashore to settle the land. They were there to catch the whales or to refit and resupply their ships. There was a ready supply of kauri wood in the north for masts and spars.

Many of the sealers and whalers were unsavory characters. They cared little about the native population. They took what they wanted by force and disregarded the local customs. The Maori were independent and proud. Sooner or later there was bound to be conflict.

One of the Maori was recruited for the crew of the sailing ship *Boyd* bound for Australia. On the return trip he was flogged for some misdemeanor—the customary punishment for the European crew. To the Maori, this not only was considered a belligerent act against the man himself but to his whole tribe as well. When the ship docked and the story was told, the punishment was revenged by the burning of the ship and the massacre of almost all the crew.

Despite some of these early acts of violence, a barter trade flourished. Vegetables and flax were traded for European tools and weapons. The Maori were paid to cut lumber needed to refurbish ships that had been at sea for months at a time. The Maori were strong and able to endure hardships, but they were proud and could be vengeful when they were not shown the respect they felt was due them.

THE ARRIVAL OF MISSIONARIES

British colonization of Australia had begun as early as 1788, but it was not until 1814 that Samuel Marsden arrived to set up a missionary post in New Zealand. Under the auspices of the Anglican Church Missionary Society (CMS), tradesmen and farmers were brought to New Zealand from England to settle the land.

The Maori hunted, farmed, and fished for food. Their staple crop was the kumara, or sweet potato. They had never grown grain as food. It is said that when the Maori first saw the grain crop cultivated by the English, they pulled it out of the ground looking for the roots to eat. When the first plow was brought to New Zealand in 1820, the Maori were angry, feeling the soil was being damaged—killed, they said.

It was the Reverend Samuel Marsden who introduced the first horses and cattle to the islands. The Maori were in awe of the huge animals. When they first saw Marsden riding a horse, they were sure he had superhuman power.

While some good was brought to the country, some of the early missionary-farmer-teachers were poor examples of Western culture. They often fought among themselves. They drank too much and some set up households with more than one native wife, enjoying the Maori's relaxed attitude toward sex that the church was trying to change.

The Maori called the whites *pakeha*, which means "colorless." Professor Lee of Cambridge University invented written Maori in the 1820s. One of the early lay missionaries and schoolteachers named Thomas Kendall is credited with compiling the first short dictionary of the Maori language. Then in 1834 William Colenso arrived with a printing press. Colenso printed Bibles and prayer books in the Maori language.

In 1835 the famous naturalist Charles Darwin arrived at the mission station at Waimate north and wrote: "On an adjoining slope fine crops of barley and wheat were standing in full ear; and in another part fields of potatoes and clover . . . There were large gardens with every fruit and vegetable which England produces."

The land had proved to be a Garden of Eden, and many of the

Reverend Samuel Marsden (left) introduced horses and cattle to New Zealand. Charles Darwin (right) visited and marveled at the fertility of the land.

truly devout missionaries hoped to keep it that way. They did not want to see New Zealand colonized. There had been too many unfortunate cases of Europeans corrupting native populations. They hoped to convert the Maori to Christianity and leave them unspoiled in their paradise.

However, news of the paradise had reached too many people on the outside. By the 1830s there was a scramble for land by European speculators. The Maori had no conception of individual ownership of land. It was held by various tribes and frequently complicated by conflicting claims of ownership among tribes. (Many deals in land transfer between pakeha and Maori are still being contested in courts today.)

Missionaries frequently tried to settle disputes peaceably, but they were not magistrates. The church kept lobbying the British government to intervene in New Zealand to establish law and order.

A group of officials in Sydney, part of New South Wales, Australia, provided what little British administrative control there was in New Zealand, but more than 1,500 miles (2,414 kilometers) separated the two landmasses. There was no practical form of government in New Zealand, at least not in the eyes of the British residents. The Maori referred to the British consul as "a man of war without guns."

By the 1830s a few thousand pakeha were living in the country. The largest settlement was in the Bay of Islands. Some of them were whalers, who tried to export their whale oil to London. But New Zealand was considered a foreign country, and all goods faced stiff custom duties. Many of these new settlers wanted a permanent connection with Britain.

There were still a number of whites, mainly missionaries, who treated the Maori with respect. They felt that the Maori should be consulted about their own future, and that if annexation should take place, it had to be done in a fair and orderly fashion. They pleaded with the British colonial office, half a world away, to offer a treaty that would put to rest the disputes over property ownership.

A TREATY IS SIGNED

The Treaty of Waitangi was drawn up and signed on February 6, 1840, with naval captain William Hobson representing the British government. The treaty called for the Maori to surrender their rule of the land in return for promised British protection, and all the rights and privileges of British subjects. The most controversial consequence of the treaty was that the Maori agreed to sell land only to the British government. That land was then

Settlers and Maori held meetings in the Maori villages.

sold to European settlers at a modest profit. There were few complaints until Britain gave the New Zealand colony substantial self-government. It was then that local officials grabbed much Maori land at cheap prices to resell on speculation. It was the start of the land wars.

Immediately following the signing of the treaty, a group of immigrants arrived from England and settled in Wellington. Others from Devon and Cornwall in England established New Plymouth. Still other immigrants turned to the South Island. Here potentially arable land was scarce and the Maori were in no mood to share. Fighting broke out. These settlers claimed to have bought land before the Treaty of Waitangi was signed.

Although the treaty had tried to protect the Maori from land-hungry Europeans, it did not settle many of the land-ownership problems. Most land was owned by the tribal community where their ancestors had settled. Much of the land was not in use and therefore not deemed valuable. When the chiefs began to sell rights to the land, they thought they were leasing the land for a fee, but this was not what the new immigrants had in mind.

The differences in what each side considered to be their rights were certain to bring on a rebellion. But there first was fighting among the tribes themselves. The "Musket Wars" lasted from the 1820s to the 1840s. Land gained by conquest was sold to Europeans by the new owners, but when Europeans turned up to claim the land, the old owners refused to vacate what they claimed was theirs. According to the treaty, no land could change hands except through a government transaction.

After twenty-five years of anarchy, the Maori had accepted the religion of the Europeans and had abandoned tribal warfare. They had learned to read and write. Their literacy rate was even higher than the pakeha. They had learned to cultivate new crops that they sold to the whites, but they had been refused any part in the establishment of self-government. The right to vote went with individual ownership of property. Since the Maori did not have individual property, they were denied the vote.

There was great rivalry between tribes. What the Maori needed was a strong leader to unite them. Such a person stepped forward in 1856 to unite the Waikato tribe. His name was William Thompson, a son of the revered Chief Waharoa. He had already made a name for himself as a peacemaker. He had established a simple code of laws, based on the Ten Commandments. He set up courts to settle disputes. In his own village he persuaded the people to build schools. He impressed everybody with his sincerity and willingness to cooperate.

In 1856 the bottom dropped out of the export wheat market. It was hard for the Maori to understand that their crops were not wanted, that grain must rot in the fields. Thompson went to Auckland to talk to the governor. He had a proposal. If the Maori were shut out of the European Parliament, they would form their

William Thompson, the son of a Maori chief, made a name for himself as a peacemaker.

own government and take care of their own problems. The pakeha did not take the threat seriously until it was too late.

A meeting was held the following year, when many chiefs from the central part of the North Island gathered to elect a king. The "King Movement" would unite the tribes under a single chief and Te Wherowhero was the chosen one. The members of his court were divided. There were moderates who felt that the Maori could well afford to be friendly to the pakeha as long as no more land was sold. And there were extremists who wished to push every white man into the sea.

*Te Kooti (left) and an artist's interpretation of
a Maori raid during the Te Kooti's War (above)*

FIGHTING BETWEEN THE MAORI AND WHITE SETTLERS

For ten years there were skirmishes between some Maori tribes
and the government. During the conflict, terrible seeds of hatred
were sown. British troops burned Maori settlements. Some Maori
renounced their Christian religion and organized a new religion
called *Pai Marire*, which literally means "good and peaceful,"
although pagan rituals of cannibalism were permitted.

Some tribes fought on the British side to pay off old scores. On
July 12, 1863, European troops invaded the Waikato stronghold of
the King Movement. Though faced with overwhelming numbers
of soldiers who were armed with heavy artillery, the Maori
continued to fight until their defeat on April 2, 1864. Other battle
areas were in the Bay of Plenty where both sides received heavy
losses. The Te Kooti's War was fought between 1868 and 1872. It
was Te Kooti, the founder of the Ringatu church, who massacred
isolated settlers as a warning to stay out of tribal territory.

The Ringatu church practiced a religion that combined the
paganism of early idol worship with Christianity. The forces of

nature were worshiped. At times there were even sacrifices of animals to appease the many gods they felt ruled their lives.

Other Maori tried to make the best of the situation by following white ways, but there was competition between Maori and pakeha farmers even when there was peace. The Maori were quick to learn a new kind of farming, marketing, and financing, but they had to struggle against the British common law system introduced to New Zealand. An individual Maori who wanted to farm property had problems proving individual ownership. That valuable piece of legal paper called a title was necessary to obtain loans from banks and merchants to buy equipment or stock.

There were still many instances of discrimination. When New Zealand first organized a responsible form of self-government patterned after the British, voting rights were distributed on an individual property-holding basis. This deprived the Maori of representation simply because no solution to the tribal property problem had been found. This was corrected to a degree with the creation of four electorate areas in the country reserved solely for the Maori. It is still true today that these four seats cannot be contested by pakeha. Other seats may be won by Maori in open elections, campaigning in districts where they now live.

There were other forms of prejudice. Some settlements refused to permit the Maori among them to practice their tribal ceremonies, their dances, and their "sings," on the grounds that heathen influences would corrupt the community. The Maori, once so fiercely proud, began to hide their heritage. Their numbers decreased because of their susceptibility to the European diseases of influenza, tuberculosis, and venereal disease.

The white settlers were so busy with their own affairs that they ignored the problems of the people they were supposed to protect.

Gold was discovered in the Arrow River in 1862. Tent cities (above) sprang up as prospectors arrived. Arrowtown (below) has been preserved as a historic area.

Chapter 3

GOLD AND WOOL

In 1861 the word gold echoed around the world. It had already brought a frenzy of fever to California in 1849. Now twelve years later, speculators flocked to central Otago on the South Island. Gabriel Read, a prospector from California, had found gold in a gully along the Tuapeka River. In just four months, four thousand men swarmed into a valley not five-miles (eight-kilometers) long.

Tent cities went up. Supplies were brought in. The population of the South Island trebled in the next decade. But sadly the mother lode, if not completely exhausted, was diminished to the point where the lure of riches was not strong enough to keep the miners working the rock and riverbeds.

The real wealth of the land was discovered in a far less dramatic way. A few farmers had already imported flocks of merino sheep from Australia. They found that the rich pastures and moderate climate of New Zealand were well adapted to raising sheep. But with their good-intentioned methods of improving the land, they almost caused catastrophe.

The strong, coarse wool from romney sheep (above) is used for making carpets (right).

When the English moved in, they cleared large tracts of land by cutting the forests and burning grasslands to make pasture for the sheep. Eventually wind and rain gouged great gullies in the high country and streams became choked with silt and gravel. It took several generations of poor management to prove to the sheep farmers, who are called run holders, that they must respect the land.

The first sheep imports from Australia were the merinos, noted for their fine wool but tough meat. Next came the romneys, great producers of fat lambs, but whose wool was coarse and strong. Today it is highly prized for use in carpets.

ECONOMIC PROBLEMS

During the worst of the depression of the 1880s, a new industry developed that was a godsend to the farmers of New Zealand. In the past, sheep had been raised almost entirely for wool and only a small amount of meat from the sheep was consumed locally.

New Zealand was just too far away from world markets to export the valuable meat product.

In 1882 a refrigerator ship, the *Dunedin*, was loaded with sheep's carcasses. It sailed from New Zealand on February 13 and arrived in England three-and-a-half months later on May 24. The voyage almost ended in disaster. The new machinery broke down several times and set fire to the sails. The captain almost froze to death trying to repair the main air duct in the freezer compartment. But the cargo arrived safely and profits were higher in England, in spite of the transportation cost, than they would have been if the meat had been sold in New Zealand.

This new export industry and the expansion of dairy products, notably cheese and butter, brought a new influx of immigrants hoping to make their fortunes. Dairy farmers imported the best stock. And it was found that a smaller farm could produce more income than the larger pastoral ranges of the run holders.

The farmers' affluence and influence grew. At the same time the government was spending money, which it borrowed from London banks, to finance capital works like railroads, harbor installations, and telegraph stations. Many workers immigrated to New Zealand at that time.

New Zealand had refused an invitation to become part of the new Commonwealth of Australia, but was upgraded in status by the British Parliament from "colony" to "dominion." This gave a boost to New Zealanders' pride.

PARLIAMENTARY GOVERNMENT

In 1865 Great Britain granted New Zealand the right to form its own government. However, executive power was still vested in the British monarch, represented by the governor-general. In practice, the governor-general had to be guided by the advice of the Cabinet, led by the prime minister.

Legislative power was first assigned to two governing bodies. However the often ineffectual upper house of Parliament, appointed by the governor-general, was abolished by practical New Zealanders. The lower house, the General Assembly, is an elected group of representatives.

The political pattern of New Zealand is similar to the British with two parties reflecting conservative and liberal policies. But because of the difference in size, geography, economy, and attitudes of the two countries, the political process in New Zealand takes on a much different style. Debates are more personal. Audiences are smaller. Economic backgrounds are not too dissimilar, which brings the parties closer together.

Auckland, the largest of the cities, tends to dominate parliamentary decisions, but elsewhere small-town politics has an important say in local government. The unions and cooperative farming organizations continue to expand their influence.

Like Britain, New Zealand uses no written constitution. What would be thought of as laws are scattered through a number of Acts of Parliament. When tradition has set the rules, it takes an overwhelming majority to vote a change. Politicians have been reluctant to take bold stands to divert the course of government. It has allowed the country a steady growth with a sense of stability.

The prime minister, the leader of the party with the most seats in Parliament, has great power. The prime minister presides over the House of Representatives, which has ninety-seven members, each elected for three-year terms.

As the prosperous reputation of the country improved over the years with a responsible government to settle crises, there were several waves of immigration. Gold had brought some, farming others, yet New Zealanders were glad to remain under the protective arm of Great Britain.

WORLD WAR I

With the coming of World War I, New Zealand's sense of nationalism rose, yet her ties with her "mother country" were bound even tighter. Between 1914 and 1918, over 100,000 New Zealanders joined the Australia-New Zealand Army Corps (ANZAC forces) and sailed for the Middle East and Europe.

By the end of the war, eighteen thousand New Zealanders had been killed in action and many thousands returned home badly wounded. The war also had been a time of unprecedented prosperity. Great Britain bought all the farm products New Zealand could produce. As a result, farmland became grossly overvalued. The period following the war was the heyday of large farm cooperatives.

New Zealand had gained the respect of the world, but she was left alone for the next few decades to mind her own business. This suited her citizens just fine. They seemed to prefer their life of moderate isolation, yet world affairs could not pass them by.

The Great Depression of the 1930s affected New Zealand as well as the great world powers. The country's economic survival depended on world markets for meat, wool, and dairy products. When prices fell, unemployment was widespread. There were riots in Auckland in April 1932.

SOCIAL REFORMS

A new Labour party took power in 1935 during the Great
Depression. The government tried to ease the problems of the
poor by passing far-reaching social legislation. Parliament passed
a full-scale social security system and a comprehensive health-
care system. The cost of medicine and doctors' care was assumed
by the government. New Zealand pioneered no-fault insurance
claims. There was to be compensation for all.

New Zealand always had fiercely asserted equal rights among
its minority population. It was the first nation to give women the
right to vote, in 1893, and there was concern that the Maori have a
say in the governing of their own land. Yet it was a curious
combination of liberal conservatism, a country supporting
individual initiative, yet willing to call on the government to step
in and "fix things up" when the economy slowed down.

WORLD WAR II

But just as New Zealand was in the midst of solving her own
problems, World War II broke out. Her strong sense of
involvement with England led New Zealand to declare war
immediately on Hitler's Germany. Again her military forces were
mobilized. This time nearly 200,000 were called for combat and
most volunteered for service.

Some of her armed forces served with General Douglas
MacArthur and Admiral Ernest J. King in the Pacific campaign,
while the majority served in North Africa, Italy, and the island of
Crete.

CHANGES AFTER WORLD WAR II

Following World War II the political climate of the country changed. The Labour party had lost much of its popularity. The National party fought for a greater private enterprise system and won the election of 1949. Most people, especially the heads of big business, thought dramatic changes would occur. Nothing much did change, and again the Labour party took control for a short time.

When again the Nationalists were voted to power, under the leadership of Prime Minister Keith Holyoake, it was surprising how many liberal ideas were added to the laws of the land. Capital punishment was abolished and a well-financed program for rehabilitation of prisoners through job education was instigated.

Holyoake also made it easy for anyone renting a state-financed housing unit to purchase the home by using as credit the amount that person had already paid in rent. There had been a shortage of houses and flats, as the New Zealanders call apartments, for a long time. Part of the problem was that there were few New Zealanders working in the building trades. Many of the qualified workers had found employment in Australia. Most of these skilled laborers had to be imported from England and The Netherlands.

OMBUDSMAN

New Zealand became the first country outside of Scandinavia to create a parliamentary commissioner, called an ombudsman, to investigate claims against bureaucracy and government. Where claims are justified, the commissioner can take immediate action, such as restoring lost pensions or moving boundary lines. When the claims are not justified, the ombudsman explains the government's position on the complaint and the case is closed. This gives the average citizen a fair chance to speak his or her case without getting involved in lengthy legal action, which can be expensive.

CHANGES IN THE 1970s

In December 1972, the first Labour government for more than twelve years came to power under the leadership of Norman Kirk. The Labour government's foreign policy stressed more independence from foreign alignment. Diplomatic relations with the People's Republic of China were established.

In the meantime, the biggest change in the economy occurred at the time Great Britain joined the European Economic Community (formerly the Common Market, now called the EEC) in 1973. Trade barriers went up for all products exported to Britain, New Zealand's major market for agricultural products. During World War II that figure had jumped to 90 percent. In return, nearly half of New Zealand's imports came from Great Britain, with most of the rest from Australia and the United States.

Suddenly the cost of industrial goods New Zealand needed to buy from abroad skyrocketed, and the amount of income-producing products she could sell to Britain and to Europe was drastically reduced by the EEC countries. In spite of the fact that New Zealand, through her efficient farming programs, could produce meat and dairy products cheaper than any other country—even including the cost of transportation—she lost out in the major markets she used to depend upon. New Zealand searched for new markets in the United States and Japan.

What brought about even more economic disaster was the rise of oil prices in the 1970s. New Zealand's farming is highly mechanized. Tractors use fuel, and so do the trucks that transport people and produce. New Zealand was forced to borrow money, which left her with a burdensome debt.

With such an economic crisis, many of the expensive government welfare programs were discontinued. Local currency was devalued. However, inflation continued. Much against the wishes of labor and business, in 1982 the Nationalist government imposed a freeze on all wages, prices, and rents. The freeze was lifted in 1984.

In 1975 severe restrictions were placed on immigration. The number of people entering the country declined from 30,000 to 5,000. Yet by the 1980s, many New Zealanders themselves were leaving the country to look for work, mainly in Australia, creating immigration in reverse. Many of the best-educated people in the country were the first ones to leave. By 1984 unemployment reached 130,000, and the national debt was $NZ 20 billion. (New Zealand's currency is the dollar.)

ENVIRONMENTAL ISSUES

Other problems were gaining international attention. Environmentalists began to lobby for important issues. Compromises had to be reached between those who wanted to dam up rushing rivers for hydroelectric power and those who wanted to preserve the natural beauty of the land. Another major concern was the use of chemicals to clear the ground for farming.

The Rainbow Warrior *was sunk in Auckland harbor in 1985.*

Perhaps the biggest battle was over the nuclear issue. France owns several small islands in the South Pacific. They used one of these islands, Mururoa, for nuclear testing. When all efforts through the United Nations failed, the New Zealand government sent a protest ship to French Polynesia to try to block the tests.

In 1985 the trawler *Rainbow Warrior,* the flagship of the international antinuclear environmentalist group Greenpeace, was to lead a flotilla to Mururoa in French Polynesia to protest against French testing of nuclear weapons in the Pacific. But before it left Auckland harbor, the *Rainbow Warrior* was blown up and sunk and one crew member was killed.

Two agents of the French secret service were arrested, convicted of manslaughter, and sentenced to ten years imprisonment. The French government made repeated requests to have the prisoners turned over to them. When the New Zealand government denied the request, the French government blocked exports to France and the other Common Market countries. A final agreement was reached where the prisoners were to be transferred to detention in the jurisdiction of France for three years. France offered a formal apology and paid compensation. Most of the money went to Greenpeace and to finance the antinuclear movement in New Zealand.

At the same time New Zealanders were entering a strong protest against nuclear-powered and armed United States vessels being permitted in New Zealand ports.

In 1986 Prime Minister David Lange of the Labour party immediately affirmed his party's pledge to ban from New Zealand ports all vessels believed to be carrying nuclear weapons or powered by nuclear energy. This caused a considerable strain in the country's relations with Australia and the United States, its partners in the ANZUS (Australia, New Zealand, and the United States) defense treaty, an agreement that both Australia and the United States would protect New Zealand's shores in case of war.

NEW ZEALAND TODAY

Today New Zealand sees its economic future as closely tied to Australia. By 1990 import-export controls for trading and all tax duties were abolished between the two countries.

There was a time at the end of the nineteenth century when many Kiwis were in favor of establishing a governing federation with Australia. Although many New Zealanders visit Australia, and some stay for many years, New Zealand wants to stand on her own, to recognize where she is different, and to be proud of her individuality and accomplishments.

Chapter 4

THE LOOK
OF THE LAND

Wellington

Fiordland National Park

A BIT OF RIVALRY

There has always been rivalry between the two islands. The first settlements were in the North Island, while later in the nineteenth century the South Island grew to be richer and more populous. But today, while the North Island is somewhat smaller, 74 percent of the population lives here—the warmer part of the country. This is where most of the Maori make their homes. No point of land is more than 68 miles (109 kilometers) from the coast, with most cities and larger towns hugging the shore.

FIORDLAND NATIONAL PARK

The South Island, which many call "the mainland," may have smaller cities, but its scenery is unquestionably more spectacular. The fiords of the southwest cut deep into the nation's largest park, the Fiordland National Park. Less than fifteen thousand years ago this region was locked in thick ice. Glaciers gouged out long, finger-shaped lakes and carved deep coastal fiords.

Opposite page: Fiordland National Park covers over forty-six hundred square miles (twelve thousand square kilometers).

Milford Sound (above) is a favorite spot for vacationers. A suspension bridge (right) is frequently part of a hikers' trail.

Milford Sound is the best known and most spectacular of these fiords. This sea canyon is walled by 10 miles (16 kilometers) of sheer cliffs rising more than a mile (1.6 kilometers) high. It can be reached either by air or along the Milford Road (Highway 94), an alpine route that cuts through some of New Zealand's most untouched country.

THE FINEST WALK IN THE WORLD

A well-marked trail has been cleared between Lake Te Anau and Milford Sound. Dwarfed by gigantic mountains, it follows a twisting track through dense forest, across alpine grassland, along white-water rivers, and past cascading waterfalls. The deeper streams are crossed by suspension bridges. Smaller ones have to

Gorge Falls at Lake Te Anau

be forded. The highest pass climbs to 3,500 feet (1,067 meters). The trail is divided into three sections with rest huts for overnight camping. Hikers must bring their own food and bedding. It is a three-day, never-to-be-forgotten experience.

The trail is in a vast area of rugged wilderness, some of which has never been thoroughly explored. Some amateur scientists are still trying to track the giant moa bird, believed to be extinct. They were encouraged by the rediscovery of the flightless takahe in 1948, after everyone was sure the bird no longer existed.

LAKE COUNTRY

New Zealand's largest lake, Te Anau, 134 square miles (347 square kilometers) of crystal water, is protected within Fiordland National Park. Because of the region's heavy rainfall, waterfalls plunge dramatically from surrounding cliffs.

53

The underground hydroelectric station (right) built at Lake Manapouri (left) has preserved the beauty of the scenery while providing power for the country.

Close by, the waters of Lake Manapouri hide a huge hydroelectric project. Beneath the lake a tunnel drops water to sea level, turning huge turbines that generate electricity. At one time there was an active protest by New Zealanders to leave the lake level alone. Instead of a dam, which would have changed the meandering shoreline and submerged the more than thirty tree-studded islets, this unique project saved the beauty of the scenery while using the power of the water to benefit the aluminum smelter at Bluff and eventually everyone in the country.

THE FAR SOUTH

Laying claim to the title of the world's southernmost city is Invercargill, situated on the Waihopai River. It was settled by William Cargill, who in 1847 set out from Scotland to establish a Free Church of Scotland settlement. Deep in the waters off its harbor lie oyster beds. Inland there are sawmills, dairy farms,

Wellington

Invercargill

Stewart Island

Interisland ferries

fields planted for the growing of grass for seed, and, of course, the ever-present flocks of sheep.

Invercargill was a busy river port during the late 1850s and 1860s, but in later years the town of Bluff took over as the principal coastal shipping port and should be given the title of southernmost city because of its location still farther down the coast. The most important feature near Bluff is the giant Tiwai Point aluminum smelter that uses the hydroelectric power from Lake Manapouri.

Separated from South Island by the waters of Foveaux Strait, Stewart Island has a beautiful scalloped 994-mile (1,600-kilometer) coastline. Much of the country's blue cod, crayfish, and oysters come from the surrounding waters. Stewart Island lies 20 miles (32 kilometers) offshore, but it can be reached by boat or by plane. It is a land set apart from the bustle of the mainland. It is rugged and wild and has many hiking trails.

A view of Queenstown from a cableway that runs between Beacon Street and the Skyline Restaurant on Bob's Peak

QUEENSTOWN

Inland from the western shore of the South Island is Queenstown. Downtown has kept the look of its gold-rush days. Today the ghost town has been revived for tourists. The scenery is magnificent. It lies in a valley on the shore of a lake and is surrounded by mountains. If anyone wants to try panning for glitter, they can easily buy or rent the simple equipment. The bigger sluice guns abandoned a century ago still can be seen. There are marked trails for hikers and boats for shooting the rapids.

Luxury high-rise hotels dominate the skyline of Queenstown. Skiing at nearby Coronet Peak is outstanding and the views from Lake Wakatipu are breathtaking.

Scenes of Queenstown: the dock at Lake Wakatipu (above), an
outdoor mall (below left), and a luxury hotel (below right)

A group of hikers on Fox Glacier

SOUTHERN ALPS

In the Southern Alps, great glaciers dig their way into the forests. Two of the most spectacular ice fields are the Fox and the Franz Josef. The color of the ice rivers vary from the blinding white of a more recent snowfall to the blue-green compacted ice, sometimes ages old, that is still accumulating and gouging out the landscape. Knowledgeable guides now lead tours across the ice fields. Only recently have roads opened up this wilderness area, but paved two-lane roads now penetrate the mountain parks: Mount Cook, Arthur's Pass, and Mount Aspiring.

Mount Cook was named *Aorangi*, the "Cloud Piercer," by the Maori. It soars 12,349 feet (3,764 meters) into the sky, dominating seventeen surrounding peaks, each but a few thousand feet lower.

Mount Cook, the highest peak on New Zealand

From its shoulders and the surrounding ranges, great glaciers push their way into the valley.

Mount Cook was first climbed on Christmas Day 1894, but the sheer Caroline Face was not conquered until 1970. There are all degrees of difficulty for the amateur climber to attempt. At the park headquarters all hikers must sign the "intentions book," so their safety can be checked. More than one hiker has been lost and had to be rescued by rangers, and some fatalities have occurred.

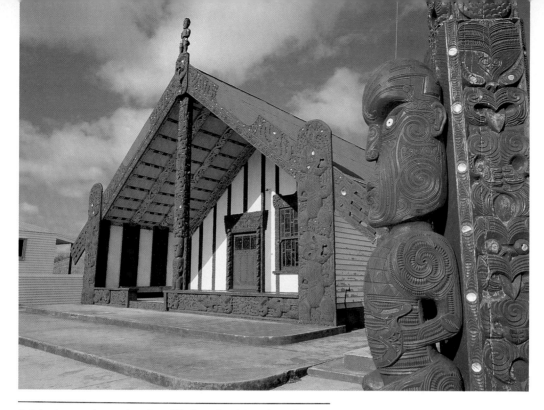

Intricate wood carving is still done by Maori craftsmen.

THE LAND OF THE GREEN STONE

The west coast of South Island has been described as rugged and it is inhabited by people of the same character. Rivers are short and rapid. Prevailing winds from across the Tasman Sea drop their moisture as they butt their energy against the wall of mountains. Forests of beech trees, native to the west coast, are of special concern to environmental groups.

There are ruins of Maori settlements here. These early residents came to mine the prized green stone for weapons and ornaments. It is still dug to make the ever-present good-luck charm, the tiki, found in many homes and tourist markets. The tiki, a grotesque gnomelike figure said to be the symbol of fertility, was used in larger-than-life size to decorate Maori meetinghouses. Small tikis for necklaces and key rings are sold to tourists.

Nelson is a thriving center for the arts.

AROUND THE TOP

Nelson, a city of some 44,000 inhabitants, is near the north edge of the South Island. It is one of the country's oldest cities. Colonists settled here in 1841. Here there are lush gardens and orchards and nearby the scenic Nelson Lakes National Park. It is both a holiday spot and a thriving center for the arts. It is particularly known for its fine pottery made from local clays.

To the east of Nelson, Marlborough Sounds makes an intricate pattern on the map. Narrow, watery fingers deeply indent the coastline. Called "The Sounds," these drowned river valleys create more than 600 miles (966 kilometers) of shoreline, a maze of sheltered waterways, inviting bays and coves, and wooded peninsulas sloping steeply to the sea. Pleasure craft now sail the waters first explored by Captain Cook more than two hundred years ago.

Docks at the port of Dunedin

DUNEDIN

The two largest cities on the South Island are Dunedin and Christchurch, both on the east coast. The older of the two is Dunedin, which was founded in 1848 by two Scottish settlers, Captain William Cargill and the Reverend Thomas Burns, a nephew of the poet Robert Burns. Spread over the hills at the head of one of the country's loveliest harbors, Dunedin was envisioned by its Scottish Presbyterian founders as the "Edinburgh of the South." It is now the center of a large sheep farming province.

Dunedin was once the chief commercial city of the nation and the jumping-off point for the gold rush in 1861. It was the wealthiest and most influential town in Victorian New Zealand. In 1869, the city fathers established the country's first university — Otago University — in Dunedin.

Many Scottish traditions are still kept alive. The country's only kilt maker and whiskey distillery are here. A statue of the Scottish poet, Robert Burns, stands in the center of the city.

The monument to sheepdogs at Lake Tekapo

MACKENZIE COUNTRY

Inland from the coast the Mackenzie Country, where they still raise merino sheep, covers a vast basin of coarse grass that is gradually being replaced by richer English varieties. It is walled in by steep mountains. The climate is harsh. Sturdy pioneers settled in the area and they brought their sheepdogs with them. Today a statue has been erected along the shores of Lake Tekapo in honor of these canine heroes that saved many a flock from scattering into the wilds, never to be seen again. A good sheepdog is a farmer's most valuable asset. Breeding them and training them is an exacting and respected profession.

The Mackenzie Country these days is crisscrossed with a network of canals that feed the water of the high country lakes into the Waitaki River system for irrigation and for power.

Above: The Seaward Kaikouras provide a dramatic backdrop for a panorama of Christchurch. Below: Children boating on the Avon River

The floral clock in Christchurch

CHRISTCHURCH

The most important city of the South Island is Christchurch. Formal gardens are planted everywhere and each year prizes are given to the the most beautiful displays. Unlike most cities in New Zealand, which have mountainous settings, Christchurch lies on the edge of the rich Canterbury Plains.

It was settled by the English and is said to be more English than any town in Great Britain. Christchurch retains many features established by its Anglican settlers. Shaded by overhanging trees, the Avon River meanders through the city, adding a note of old-world gracious charm. The city has the look of an English countryside.

The English planted oak, willows, and horse chestnut trees and bushes like gorse and blackberry, intended for hedges that

Christchurch Cathedral was begun in 1864 and completed in 1904.

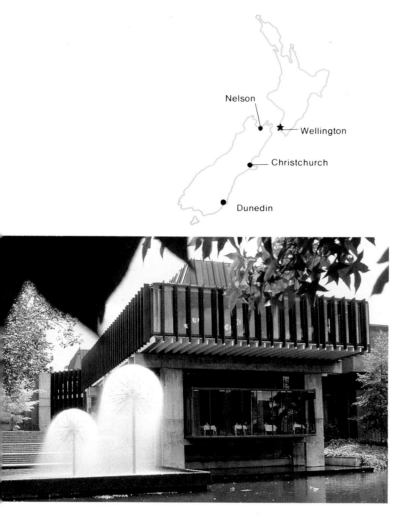

The new City Hall (left) and a shopping area (right) in downtown Christchurch

reminded them of Britain. They became so involved in creating another Britain that they even erected public buildings with all the main windows facing south. But, in the Southern Hemisphere they should have reversed the direction to take advantage of the sun.

In the very center of the city is the lofty neo-Gothic Anglican Christchurch Cathedral. The first immigrants came with the explicit intention of founding an Anglican community. To qualify for the privilege of settling a new world, all applicants had to be sober, industrious, honest, respectable citizens, and members in good standing of their church. The first four ships arrived in 1850.

The harbor and city of Wellington

WELLINGTON ON NORTH ISLAND

Across narrow Cook Strait, which divides the islands, is the capital of New Zealand—Wellington. Cook Strait is one of the most treacherous twelve miles (nineteen kilometers) of open water in the world. According to legend the Polynesian god of wind and storm—Tawhiri-ma-tea—fought most of his fiercest battles here.

Wellington is built on the splendid harbor of Port Nicholson, on the very southwest tip of North Island. Wooded hills curve like a green amphitheater around the city. Houses are scattered on the steep green slopes that overlook the bay. Most of the houses are

*An expressway (left) cuts through the city;
apartments on the harbor (right) in Wellington*

constructed of timber. One government building erected in 1876
claims to be the second-largest wooden building in the world.
Although many new buildings have been built of cement in the
downtown business center, the earlier "wedding cake" Victorian
models give charm to the capital. To the settlers wood was cheap
and stone or brick expensive.

The area lies directly across one of the most active fault lines.
The land has been grating against itself in sudden shudders since
people first settled here. In 1848 and 1855 earthquakes thrust the
land upward 5 feet (1.5 meters), which made a peninsula out of
the former island called Miramar.

Newer buildings are being built of glass and steel, and have not
been tested yet by a major earthquake. The new circular Cabinet

Wellington

The Beehive

office building, known as the Beehive, was built in the late 1970s, in contrast to the nearby impressive neoclassical marble parliamentary buildings and the neo-Gothic Assembly Library. The parliamentary chambers are modeled on those of Westminster in London. Wellington has samples of every imaginable style of architecture.

The city's climate is generally free from extremes of hot and cold. Brisk winds that funnel through Cook Strait clear the air and eliminate winter humidity that other areas experience. Yet on weekends those who are affluent enough to afford a second

There is no fog, smog, or pollution in Wellington. The air is cleared by strong winds that blow through Cook Strait.

residence head either over the hills or up the coast, where boating and water sports can be enjoyed in calmer waters. The broad valley of Hutt has absorbed much of the city's expansion during the past thirty years.

The curve of the Tasman coastline arching north from Wellington offers a fine stretch of sandy beach for the people living in the area. Farther north the Manawatu area opens up into a broad plain, which supports some of the finest breeding stock for the "lambing" farmers.

Mount Egmont

MOUNT EGMONT

Though not as dramatic as the South Island, the North Island can offer a far greater variety of scenic beauty. To the west of the province of Taranaki is the near perfect volcanic cone of Mount Egmont, known as New Zealand's Mount Fujiyama. It is a dormant volcano rising to 8,260 feet (2,518 meters), that last erupted about two hundred years ago. The Maori name is Taranaki.

The Egmont National Park encompasses the mountaintop and its densely wooded slopes, popular with vacationers in the summer and in winter. Mountain guest houses offer simple family-style accommodations for visitors.

Drizzle or mist can be present even when the sun is shining. Because of the great variations in rainfall and altitude, the slopes

Mount Ngauruhoe in Tongariro National Park is a mildly active volcano.

support an unusually varied assortment of plant life, some found only here. Dozens of rhododendrons in all colors make it a showy garden place.

The mountain stands alone in all its glory, but rich farmland extends right up to its base. The soil is rich from old volcanic ash and the climate is helped by the moisture-laden westerly breezes. Dairy cows outnumber the sheep in this area.

KING COUNTRY

In the middle of the island is Tongariro National Park. Here there are several mildly active volcanoes, the tallest being Ruapehu at 9,175 feet (2,797 meters).

The King Country lies inland. It is a bleak and rugged land with a fierce history. It was here that the Maori tried to stop the

Farms near Hamilton

encroachment of European settlers by organizing tribes into a nation and appointing a king. Maori King Te Wherowhero ruled as an independent monarch for several years. No pakeha were permitted in his kingdom.

When a truce was finally agreed upon, the land was surveyed and formally granted to the people in possession of it. In more recent times land has been sold or leased to white farmers, but still there is a sense of isolation among the large tracts of virgin forest.

There are not too many traces of civilization here, yet not much farther up the coast are the fertile valleys of Waikato where some of the finest dairy herds are raised.

HAMILTON

Hamilton, in the hub of the Waikato plains, straddles the Waikato River about 85 miles (137 kilometers) south of Auckland. It is New Zealand's largest inland city. Hamilton was established as a military settlement in 1864, but it has developed into a busy farming and agricultural research center.

A panorama of Auckland

AUCKLAND

Auckland is the largest city, port, and industrial center of New Zealand. Thanks to its superb setting—almost surrounded by water—and to the Aucklanders' love of broad boulevards and lavish flower gardens, it is a big city that has not lost its scenic beauty. Its climate is subtropical. Volcanic cones and islands rise around and even in it. The 644 feet (196 meters) of the extinct Mount Eden rise up right in the middle of town.

Auckland is a city with an important history for all races of settlers. Rivers emptying into the harbor were canoe highways for the Maori. At one time or another, every volcanic cone in Auckland was the site of a fortified Maori village. Mount Eden still bears traces of terraces and wooden palisades that protected hundreds of warriors and families just two centuries ago.

Albert Park Gardens (above) and Queen Street (below) in downtown Auckland

Harbour Bridge (left); charming old buildings that have been turned into a shopping area (right)

At the entrance to King's Wharf is a simple rock with a metal inscription marking the spot where Auckland's founder and New Zealand's first governor, Captain William Hobson, declared the settlement to be the capital of the country.

A 3,300-foot (1,006-meter) long bridge, completed in 1959, spans Waitemata Harbour. It provides commuters from the prosperous north shore a shortcut to downtown Auckland. The mouth of the harbor is protected by a number of offshore islands dominated by 854-foot (260-meter) high Rangitoto Island.

Auckland is a modern city with tall glass buildings and a tangle of traffic. But it is a sprawling city with a large urban area that spreads fifty miles (eighty kilometers) along the coast from Whangaparaoa in the north to Drury in the south. New Zealanders have been noted as having a desire "to put down a house and garden on a quarter-acre section." Here there is plenty of scenic coast to settle. Hence the city has been described as a collection of small villages.

The Bay of Islands

THE WINTERLESS NORTH

Past Auckland, a narrow peninsula of land extends some 280 miles (451 kilometers) northwest to rocky Cape Reinga. Here a sacred pohutukawa tree stands on the island's farthest rock. According to Maori legend, the spirits of departing Maori pass down the exposed roots and into the sea on their underwater return voyage to their ancestral homeland of Hawaiki. This is the land called the "winterless north."

On the west coast is a huge sweep of beach, 90 miles (145 kilometers) in all, where one of New Zealand's most sought-after table delicacies is found—the toheroa shellfish.

On the east coast of the peninsula is the Bay of Islands, site of the first European settlement and the place where the Treaty of Waitangi was signed. It is a large harbor dotted with islands. The biggest measures fifty-four acres (twenty-two hectares). The smallest is a mere rock jutting from the ocean. It is a perfect spot for tourists and sailors. Game fish attract sport fishermen.

Tourists come from all over the world to marvel at New Zealand's geysers (right) and, sometimes, to soak their feet in the hot springs (left).

ROTORUA: THE VOLCANIC PLATEAU

To the west and south of Auckland is an area known the world over for the boiling, steaming action of underground thermal activity around Wairakei and Lake Rotorua. There are only three areas in the world where geysers are found: in New Zealand at Rotorua, in Iceland, and in Yellowstone Park in the United States.

The urban area of Rotorua is home to about 58,500 people, but tourists swell that number. Around the city a thousand hot springs bubble and gush in backyards and public parks. Heavy clouds of sulfurous steam block the sunlight, but no one seems to mind. People come from all over the world to soak away their ills in the city's thermal baths. White pumice and golden sulfur combine to shape bizarre formations around the springs.

79

*Cathedral Cove Lookout
on the
Coromandel Peninsula*

BAY OF PLENTY

The Coromandel Peninsula juts like a giant hook from the south Auckland coastline. To the east it is pounded by Pacific surf, while to the west lies the sheltered Hauraki Gulf.

Swinging south is the Bay of Plenty, which was named by its first European visitor, Captain Cook. It is a place where thousands come during Christmas vacation. There is less rainfall here than in most other areas, due to the placement of the mountain ranges that squeeze the moisture from the sky before it gets to the eastern coast.

The Raukumara Range overlooks the Bay of Plenty. Here is some of the most spectacular and strangely beautiful scenery of New Zealand. There are great forests of the punga, or giant tree ferns, and, during the Christmas season, brilliant splashes of scarlet blossoms from the pohutukawa trees.

Farther south on the east coast of North Island, the land again swings in a giant curve at Hawke Bay. The twin cities of Napier and Hastings serve the rich plains, which produce vast quantities

Vineyards (left) and a cherry orchard (right) in the Hawke Bay area

of fruit and vegetables, grapes for wine, and sheep for their wool and meat.

GLOWWORM CAVES

Another tourist attraction close by are the celebrated Waitomo limestone caves, which are lit by thousands of tiny glowworms that give off a phosphorescent light shimmering from the ceiling of the caves. Tourists descend on the well-marked paths to board small boats on the underground waters that take them to the caves.

THE LAND OF NEW ZEALAND

Natural forces are still shaping the land, from beneath the surface to the tallest mountains. In 1931, Napier and Hastings were badly damaged by earthquakes. This led to some of the stringent anti-earthquake building codes of today. It is a new land, not yet worn away, and it is ever changing.

The Maori were the first settlers in New Zealand. Although they uphold their traditional ways, most also enthusiastically take part in contemporary activities, such as the skydiver at left.

Chapter 5

MAORI WAYS

CITY LIFE FOR SOME

In the space of little over a hundred years, the Maori have gone from being a majority to being a minority in the land they discovered and colonized. Thirty years ago most Maori lived in remote "native" villages, far from the pakeha's cities. By the mid-1970s, 75 percent lived in urban areas. Most Maori are unskilled, but some are entering business and professions in small, but increasing, numbers. Unfortunately New Zealand's economy doesn't need unskilled labor.

In some cases the move to urban areas has caused extreme hardships for the Maori. Their living style changed completely. They were crowded into smaller quarters than they had been used to and frequently separated from relatives who had played an important part in family life. It was feared that the younger generation of Maori were losing pride in their heritage. Youngsters joined gangs and crime rates increased alarmingly in the cities. Many felt that a strong link to their former way of life was the only solution to stem this trend.

Those who have moved to the cities do not reject their tribal homes. The fact that city dwellers own a share of land—however small—in their home district creates ties to that place, gives them the rights of the land, and establishes a sense of continuity with their cultural past. For the Maori it is the social role of the land, rather than what it can produce, that is important.

While they have assimilated many European ways—they wear Western clothing, and the majority speak English and are members of Christian churches—the Maori have not ignored their Polynesian past.

MYTH AND LEGEND

Maori culture is rich in myth and legend. These tell of the creation of the universe and of gods becoming human. They describe the coming of their people to the land they call Aotearoa. All this has been woven into oral literature, etched into carvings, and acted in song and dance that has been passed on and adapted by each generation.

One cannot be absolutely sure that all Maori are descended from those who set out in seven canoes to find a new land. Discovery may have come more gradually at different times in history, but the accuracy of some of their tales cannot be disputed.

For example, some legends tell of Kupe, a Polynesian hero credited with being among the first to sight Aotearoa. He was chasing a *wheke* (octopus) all the way from his home in Hawaiki after it had stripped bait from his fishing line. Kupe chased the octopus along the Wairarapa coast and into Cook Strait. The story gives such accurate navigational details that it provides an oral map of the Marlborough Sounds.

Maori, such as this tourist guide, enjoy telling their legends and history.

Another story tells of a canoe having been wrecked on a reef. Survivors were washed ashore and headed inland. The outline of the mountain peaks are described and named. Mount Cook was called Paki, the name of a boy who was carried on his grandfather's shoulders and was thus the tallest of all. Again the story of the overland journey gives so many details that no one trying to retrace the trip who had heard the directions could be lost.

LITERATURE

Maori literature is in three forms: narrative prose, poetry, and genealogical history. The recital of genealogy is the most highly developed. It was important to know one's roots and to honor one's ancestors. Without a written record, everything had to be stored in memory. Recital of the family tree invariably ends with the names of *Rangi* (sky) and *Papa* (earth), the marriage of which produced the gods, who in turn produced all life.

Maori poetry is always sung or chanted, the rhythm making it easier to memorize. Today speech making is a highly prized accomplishment. Maori now have a written language that was translated for them by whites, but it is the delivery of the words that puts meaning into them. The gap between spoken and written Maori is much wider than that between spoken and written English.

CEREMONIES

A wedding, funeral, or christening follows ancestral traditions. Songs and speeches in the Maori tongue bring back stories of the past. There is an openness about expressing joy and sorrow that is sometimes supressed by a pakeha. Woven into their religion are concepts of *tapu* (sacredness). There are ceremonials, especially the *hui* (gathering), the *tangi* (mourning), and *karakia* (prayer services).

Every Maori community has a ceremonial center, the *marae*. The marae consists of the meetinghouse—*whare hui*—the open ground before it, and an adjoining hall and kitchen. The meetinghouse has a certain degree of sacredness. Eating within it is strictly forbidden. It is a one-room wooden building, sometimes elaborately carved, with posts shaped in the form of the ritual tiki figure.

Gatherings are usually held in the courtyard of the meetinghouses under the supervision of the *tangata whenua*, or host tribe. Visitors are called forward with a *karanga*, a long wailing call that speaks to the living and commemorates the dead. This is performed by women only.

Answering the call, the visitors, led by their own women, come forward in single file. Then follows the ritual weeping for the dead on both sides. This is followed by the speeches of welcome

Tourists are welcome in the Maori meetinghouses.

made by the male elders. At the end of each speech, members of the host tribe get to their feet and join in a *waiata* (song). These formalities over, the visitors come forward and press noses— *hongi*—a form of ritual greeting that shows friendship and mutual respect.

FEASTS

The hui will then take up matters of local importance, often land issues that are still being disputed or perhaps issues of agricultural interest. Huge feasts are prepared. Meat and vegetables are steamed in a *hangi* (earth oven). Many kinds of seafood will be offered, such as shellfish, *kina* (sea egg), eel, and dried shark. Fermented corn is a specialty. The bread served is similar to a fried doughnut. Sharing food together is a ritual means of sharing common concerns and showing friendship.

Maori male dancers, with their faces painted, act out a story.

Dancing is almost always part of the entertainment. Men and women both take part. Dressed in the style of their ancestors with fringed, striped skirts, each group of dancers acts out a graceful, sometimes frantic, style of "hula." Men paint their faces in spiral patterns that were once permanently tattooed into their skin. Women sometimes have a *moko* (a type of tattoo) on their chins.

Male dancers often act out war games by lunging at each other with clubs, tongues stuck out in defiance. Stamping feet beat out the rhythm. One of the women's favorite dances combines hip movement and the swinging of fiber balls attached to long cords, which they whip around their heads and back and forth in front of them.

The rhythmic swinging of fiber balls on cords is part of this dance, a favorite of Maori women.

War canoes sometimes are raced tribe against tribe, but although the competition is frantic, the outcome does not provoke a battle as in the past.

Pakeha are no longer trying to impose Western culture on the Maori to "civilize" them. But it has taken pakeha several generations to appreciate and understand a culture so alien to their own background. There is beauty and deep meaning in the ways of the past, but it must be remembered that the beauty was once combined with such practices as cannibalism and slavery.

LEADERS

One of the great late nineteenth-century leaders of the Maori—Sir Apirana Ngata—served in the Parliament and did much to preserve the traditions of his people. For his role as minister of native affairs he was knighted by the New Zealand government. He sponsored legislation that helped develop Maori land, establish schools, and initiate the building of meetinghouses used for Maori community affairs. He was followed by others who saw the need to promote modern technology without destroying the patterns of the past.

Today leadership of the Maori people is disputed between the traditional chiefs of the tribes and the young, educated, radical Maori of urban background who attract much media attention.

DISCRIMINATION

Following World War II a decided change came about. Before that time few pakeha had ever known a Maori personally. Theirs was a separate community and way of life. In 1945 more than 80 percent of Maori lived in rural areas. By the 1980s, that had completely changed. For the first time these two races with different cultures were living side by side.

New Zealand has been trying to avoid the racial discrimination and bitterness that has affected other communities with minority racial mixes. There is a kind of paternalism the whites feel toward the Maori. The frequently expressed view that Maori are equal to whites has, in fact, little more meaning than that they are not actively discriminated against. But statistics prove that there is a decided gap between the two races on income earned.

Hope for improvement will come gradually through the determination of individuals to right the situation. Some pakeha are finally learning to speak the Maori language, and there have been happy intermarriages between the two races.

The kiwi fruit

Chapter 6

EVERYDAY LIFE

THE PEOPLE KNOWN AS KIWIS

What do you call a citizen of New Zealand? Well, they will answer to the term New Zealander, but you also will frequently hear them called "En Zedder." "Zed," rather than "zee," is the New Zealand way of pronouncing the last letter of the alphabet.

For a nickname the people have chosen "Kiwi," the name of a bird found only in the islands. It is a flightless bird, about the size of a chicken, and emerges only at night from its burrows in the ground to look for worms and insects. It is related to the giant moa that once roamed the land. Most En Zedders have never seen the bird except in a zoo, but because it is distinct and rare, it suits the New Zealanders.

The term should not be confused with the kiwi fruit, which is grown on the islands. The fruit was named kiwi to make it recognizable as a product of New Zealand. The fruit used to be called "Chinese gooseberry."

A DIFFERENT VOCABULARY

Too many people confuse a New Zealander with an Australian. Although they possess much in common, they are friendly rivals and guard their national identities.

There are certain phrases that only a Kiwi would use. A garage that handles body work on a car is a "panel beater." A "hogget" has nothing to do with hogs; it is a young unshorn sheep that is no longer a lamb.

There is a wonderful phrase—"Ah, yes!"—that is used after someone answers your questions or addresses a statement to you. It never conveys doubt like "Oh, yeah?" It expresses acknowledgment, interest, and a warm sense of friendship between speaker and listener.

POPULATION DISTRIBUTION

At one time Kiwis were pictured as typically country folk, living in isolation. In reality more than 2 million of the 3.3 million New Zealanders live in or close to major cities. The two largest urban areas are in the North Island, which is dominated by the residents of Auckland. In the last thirty years, Auckland has doubled its population. Its prosperity is based on the large and fertile dairy farms and pastures that surround the urban sprawl. In contrast, Wellington serves as a base for a rugged, much poorer land used for sheep.

In the South Island, more than one-fourth of the people live in the plains city of Christchurch. About one-eighth live in Dunedin, which has been declining in relative size and importance.

After the four main centers comes a group of provincial cities

*Inspectors in a meat packing plant (left)
and sheepskin rugs (above) for sale*

that act as service centers for one of the pockets of fertile coastal
or inland plains. Most are ports and have populations between
50 and 100 thousand. Although only about 10.9 percent of the
country's labor force is employed directly on farms, its cities exist
not so much for industry or manufacturing, but as a service to the
farmers. It is here where the produce from the farms is
processed—producing products such as wool, pulp wood, and fine
cuts of meat.

A YOUNG COUNTRY

New Zealand is a young country, an infant compared to any
other civilized country in the world. The United States had won
her independence and fought several wars before settlers came to
New Zealand to build homes.

Some people have called New Zealand an empty country
because about one-fourth of the population lives in Auckland. The

density of population in the rest of the country *averages* only thirty-two people per square mile (thirteen people per square kilometer), a fact for which New Zealanders express pride.

It also has been said that New Zealand is the most isolated civilized country in the world. Before jet travel, there were few who had the time or the money for the long journey to ancestral homes in the British Isles. This is probably one reason their sentimental attachment to ancestral roots had to be satisfied by building a look-alike environment to "back home."

Most forget that Auckland is 1,180 miles (1,899 kilometers) from Sydney, Australia, and five times as far from any major Western city. Yet in spite of her isolation New Zealand has taken an increasing interest in international affairs. During both world wars her fighting forces fought side by side with her European allies. New Zealand also was a founding member of the United Nations and was a member of the Southeast Asia Treaty Organization (SEATO), which ended in 1977.

NEW IMMIGRANTS

It is obvious that the majority of Europeans who came to New Zealand less than two hundred years ago were of British origin, but other races have mixed in the Kiwi melting pot. Italians came as fishermen. Yugoslavs planted vineyards. Dutch—known as conscientious workers—were encouraged to migrate after World War II. Even some Chinese, who originally came for the gold rushes, have come to swell the labor force. Scandanavians worked in the central North Island in the lumber industry. There is a good-sized Indian community and since World War II, Polish, Hungarian, Vietnamese, and Cambodian refugees have arrived.

A shepherd's family enjoys a coffee break (top left), Morris dancers in Christchurch (top right), students from Christ's College (left), and a rural family (above)

OTHER ISLANDERS WHO HAVE COME TO STAY

More recently there has been a large influx of people from other Pacific islands, particularly from Western Samoa and Cook Islands. Today Auckland is by far the largest Polynesian city in the world. Over 100,000 Maori and other Pacific Islanders make their home here. The Pacific Islanders arrived during the years of economic good times and took over the menial jobs that New Zealanders did not want to do. They have stayed, are raising their families, and are slowly earning the right to better jobs.

This has put the Maori in an odd position. They are a minority group striving to better the living conditions of their people, but now other minorities are flooding the cities. Maori leaders have been asking for special treatment from the pakeha to raise their standard of living. But now they are having to compete with newcomers.

All Polynesian cultures share a basic common language, which can vary considerably from one geographic area to another, but allows them to understand each other. Although they shared a common background generations ago, they now have distinctive cultural habits that set them apart. To bring these people together in a cohesive, fairly governed family is not an easy task.

New Zealanders have always prided themselves on their lack of discrimination, but the actions of those who preach equality must go beyond tolerance. There must be a positive understanding, appreciation, and respect of cultural differences. Many urban Maori radicals demand a bicultural society, separating divergent ethnic groups, whereas, given the racial mix, majority opinion seems to favor a multicultural society where differences are put aside.

A TIME OF CHANGE

New Zealand's culture is neither Polynesian nor European. It is a distinctive character of its own and it is constantly changing. One of the reasons the changes have come so rapidly is the growth of the tourist industry. New Zealand is within reach of any place in the world within a matter of hours now, and the country is welcoming visitors.

In 1960 it was difficult to find a restaurant outside of a hotel, and only hotel restaurants served wine or liquor. Most Kiwis entertained at home. Now there are hundreds of ethnic restaurants catering to cosmopolitan tastes.

Until the beginning of the 1980s, all shops were closed from Friday evening to Monday morning. Now they are open on Saturdays to accommodate visitors who frequently come on guided tours with only a few days to explore the whole country.

For 150 years there was a leveling of status and income within the country. Today there is more competition and a growing division between rich and poor. This is causing more problems than the government can possibly solve at one time, but they are conscientiously trying. However, unemployment is increasing at an alarming rate.

EDUCATION

New Zealand is a combination of free enterprise and state socialism designed to help bring about equality of opportunity by offering equality of education. Theoretically this will take care of any imbalance of political, social, or racial prejudice.

The Maori have been regarded by anthropologists as among the

An elementary school classroom

most advanced aboriginal races of the Pacific. There is no gulf between the races in respect to intelligence, but the statistics show that a smaller percentage of Maori enroll in university classes than do pakeha. The government has been sponsoring a public relations campaign that stresses higher education for all as an investment in the future.

Kiwis are proud of the fact that New Zealand offers universal education from age five to nineteen for every person who seeks it, and university education, which is virtually free, to all who qualify for it. There also are fine private schools, which are growing in popularity. The best known is Christ's College in Christchurch.

Ever since the passing of the Education Act of 1877, popular education has been stressed as a means of getting ahead. Public

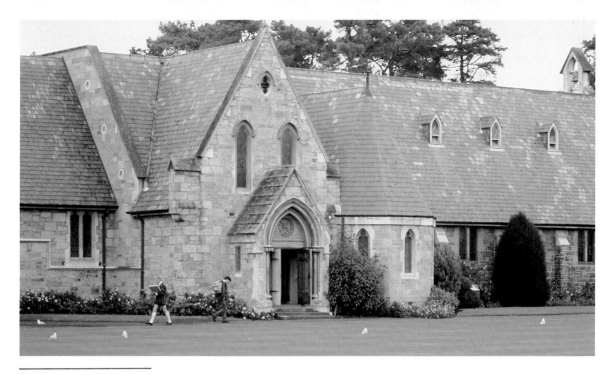

Christ's College

schools operate without discrimination as to race, religion, or wealth. All children—whether they live in luxury, in an urban tenement, or in the rural hinterland—study the same curriculum.

KINDERGARTEN TO COLLEGE

The first free kindergarten was started in 1889 in Dunedin for all children. It was recognized that early training had a distinct influence on future success in education.

In today's school system, the average primary school pupil passes through the first four *forms* in a little over six years, entering secondary education at age thirteen plus. Parents are free to choose for their child the school and course deemed most desirable and suitable.

Even for those who are geographically isolated from community schools, there is help. Correspondence lessons are mailed weekly, and audiocassettes are available. To give these students a sense of being a part of a group studying the same course, they are given badges and uniforms. A printed magazine keeps track of different news items from this scattered student body. Traveling teachers come to visit at least once a semester.

The latest statistics show that 94 percent of the school-age population are enrolled in some form of curriculum.

There are six universities, an agricultural college with university status, and teacher-training colleges, as well as twenty-two polytechnical institutions offering education at the post-secondary level.

New Zealand has four universities that offer advanced courses in all subjects. With the agricultural emphasis of its population, it is only natural that much of its efforts are directed toward research in crop and animal development.

Expenditures by the central government on education represent about 12.4 percent of the total spending on all programs, an effort unequaled in many other countries. New Zealand is truly planning for the future.

THE ARTS

New Zealand is a country so physically isolated from the rest of the world and tied so strongly to a conservative heritage that their art has often been a copy of trends. There have been few great innovators, yet when talent was recognized it surpassed competition.

Those who have made a name for themselves have often done it first abroad. Painter Frances Hodgkins, writer Katherine Mansfield, and opera star Kiri te Kanawa are famous internationally as well as in their place of birth.

Contemporary stained-glass art

Because so much of the population is centered around one or two large cities, there are few theaters for the performing arts in smaller communities, yet those that do exist have enthusiastic audiences. Auckland has a thriving cultural life, as does Wellington and Christchurch. Auckland is proud of its symphony orchestra, professional theater, and ballet company. The city of Christchurch also has choral groups that perform regularly.

New Zealanders must be among the best-read people in the world. Statistics show that they spend about $NZ 60 per person a year purchasing books.

CRAFTS

Crafts have been an important form of expression since pioneer days. Today there is a large community of artists working in the fields of glassblowing, stained-glass imagery, and pottery. Wood carving in ancient and contemporary styles is seen everywhere. And of course, with such an abundance of the natural product,

A Maori artist painting his hand-carved panel

hand-woven and knitted items and sheepskin and leather products are prized buys for tourists.

INVENTIVE TALENT

New Zealand has intentionally avoided nuclear energy technology, yet New Zealand-born Lord Ernest Rutherford is considered one of the great scientists in the early development of nuclear research.

Kiwis have often proved their ingenious ability to invent things on their own, using the most basic of tools. It has been said they are "make do" geniuses. Richard Pearse, a South Canterbury farmer working entirely alone, came within days of beating the Wright brothers into the air with a machine largely fashioned from flattened out sheep-dip tins.

SPORTS

Kiwis are among the most sports-minded people of any country in the world. Some say this is because they live surrounded by a rugged terrain that has yet to be tamed. The country presents challenges, and New Zealanders have accepted the challenges in competitive ways.

New Zealand was founded by people who braved the sea in primitive canoes and later in sailing ships. Descendants today have kept traditions alive by using the water for sport and recreation.

Maori still race their war canoes. These boats are skillfully crafted and decorated as works of art. The skills of the builders have been passed from one generation to another. Master artisans are as honored as the crews who win the races.

Many pakeha choose to sail the waters under canvas. Sailors in all size craft—from the beautiful *New Zealand* that competed in the 1988 Americas Cup race to the smallest sailing dinghy—compete for fun and honor. The Auckland Anniversary Regatta, with more than one thousand entries, is the biggest one-day yachting event in the world.

New Zealand teams have won many world championship rowing contests and have collected Olympic gold medals.

Rivers tumbling from mountains in the interior have taxed the ability of world-class, white-water kayakers, canoeists, and rafters.

FISHING AND DIVING

A country bounded by water and laced by streams is bound to be a fisherman's paradise. Some of the best freshwater fishing draws anglers from around the world to New Zealand's lakes and streams. Renowned for its trout fishing, Lake Rotoiti is a favorite. An average New Zealand trout weighs 3.5 pounds (1.6 kilograms). If fact, if you want to eat trout in this country, you'll have to catch it yourself. There is a law against catching trout commercially.

And to impress deep-sea fishing experts, even one that got away made *The Guinness Book of Records.* A huge broad bill was hooked and played for over thirty-one miles (fifty kilometers), towing the boat, before the line snapped. Someone took pictures and timed the event, so that jealous outsiders could not doubt the Kiwi feat.

The unique underwater seascape surrounding New Zealand makes scuba diving, both a scientific and recreational sport, an important activity. Some unique species are found only in these waters.

MOUNTAINEERING AND SKIING

Mountaineering is probably this country's best-known outdoor sport. It was Sir Edmund Hillary, a native son, who was the first to climb Mount Everest. New Zealand's mountains cannot match the height of the Himalaya, but their treacherous head walls make this a good training ground. Rock falls are common. Fast-moving glaciers are split with crevasses and swept with avalanches. The weather comes from across a stormy western sea that can change a sunny day into a howling blizzard.

In winter the mountains are a haven for skiers as well as climbers. Some of the slopes have lifts and facilities equal to those in Europe and North America, but New Zealanders pride themselves on tougher going. Ski mountaineering is a fast-

The thrills of mountaineering (left) and hang gliding (right) appeal to New Zealanders.

growing sport. Some fields can be reached only by a long climb with skis and food on one's back or shoulder. There are places where huts are provided for overnight shelter. Some adventurous skiers take along tents to spend a week or more skiing in unmarked snow.

In commercial resorts helicopters and ski planes whisk skiers to the top of the runs, and small mountain lakes form natural skating rinks. When the snow wears thin, the risk takers try hang gliding.

CAMPING

Camping is almost a national way of life during the summer months. This is probably why resort hotels have only recently been built and are popular mainly with foreign visitors. National parks, some even close to cities, offer magnificent scenery and recreation.

RUGBY—THE NATIONAL SPECTATOR SPORT

Rugby is the national spectator sport. It is a game a little like soccer and a lot like American football. The players do not wear heavy padding and can move faster in a sort of gridiron ballet, passing the ball until grounded with bone-jarring tackles.

The national team is known as the All Blacks, because of their black jerseys and shorts. They have a regular schedule of matches on home fields and abroad.

Teams from other countries are invited to compete in test matches, and games for the home teams are held between different clubs. It is almost impossible to get one of the fifty thousand seats in the Auckland stadium during the height of the season.

CRICKET

Cricket is a sport that has been adopted from the British. It often can be a long and complicated game to follow and a spectator who doesn't know the rules can become very confused.

RUNNING

Long-distance running races have been popular in New Zealand ever since two of her best—Peter Snell and Murray Halberg—won medals in the 1960 Olympics. Now in almost any month of the year, marathon races are held.

WINNERS

Individual honors have been won in many sports by Kiwis:

New Zealanders make contests out of everything, including dangerous-looking wood-chopping contests.

Dennis Hulme, racing car driver; Bob Fitzsimmons, boxer; and Anthony Wilding, tennis star.

New Zealanders tend to make contests out of everything from wood chopping to sheep shearing, and every contestant has his or her hometown cheering section.

HORSE RACING

Horse racing has developed into big business. Almost every city has a track, complete with a grandstand for the spectators who jam the park. The courses are some of the finest anywhere, and as for numbers, tiny New Zealand boasts more horses and racecourses per capita than any other country in the world.

With its natural advantage of a temperate climate and limestone-rich soil that produces lush pastures, New Zealand has proved to be an excellent thoroughbred nursery. Her champions have been exported for stud duty all over the world.

New Zealand's neighbor Australia offers higher stakes for racing winners, but local breeders have more races they can enter each year.

The Wairakei geothermal power station uses natural
steam, formed underground, to produce electricity.

Chapter 7

COMMERCE AND INDUSTRY

NATURAL ASSETS

New Zealand has always been poor in mineral assets. The first European mining was for gold, then manganese and copper. Deposits were too small for substantial profit. In the mid-1800s, explorer Thomas Brunner found coal in the South Island.

SOURCES OF ENERGY

New Zealand's real wealth lies in its abundance of energy. There is a coal-burning station producing electricity at Meremere and several huge hydroelectric systems using the ample supply of whitewater rivers, especially in South Island.

Another type of energy comes from the ground. New Zealand is one of the few countries in the world where molten lava is so close to the surface that it heats groundwater to steam. In the Wairakei area these steam geysers are capped to produce power, which not only heats homes but brings electricity to homes and businesses.

A modest gas field off the west coast of North Island has been discovered. It will help expand the sources of energy for the growing light industry New Zealand is trying to develop.

In 1969 the country's first deep oil well was drilled 33 miles (53 kilometers) offshore in 360 feet (110 meters) of water. A modest-sized refinery was built, which is saving several million dollars in foreign exchange.

MANUFACTURING

The power from the hydroelectric plant under Lake Manapouri fuels the large Comalco aluminum smelter plant near Invercargill. Tremendous heat is needed to process the raw product bauxite, which is shipped from Queensland, Australia. When the ore is finally processed into ingots, it is sold to manufacturing plants all over the world. This also helps New Zealand balance her foreign-trade deficit.

Just south of Auckland a new steel mill has been built. It fills most of New Zealand's local needs. The country has been slow to develop any large-scale industry except that which involves agricultural produce. The industries that have succeeded typically specialize in "short run" production, which giant industries in Japan and the United States find too costly to produce.

A glassworks and a nylon spinning factory have been built. A cotton mill was partially constructed some years ago, but opposition from textile importers canceled the project.

New Zealand does not manufacture standard automobiles. Since imports are heavily taxed, they are expensive. Tractors and heavy farm machines are imported. Most milling equipment is manufactured in New Zealand.

There are more sheep than people in New Zealand.

NONMETALLIC MINERALS

Although the search for base metals in New Zealand has been largely fruitless, the country has a good supply of important nonmetallic minerals, such as clay, limestone, sand, and gravel used to make agricultural lime, cement, and glass. Other minerals of importance are serpentine and a low-grade phosphate rock used in fertilizer production.

Industrial salt has been produced from minerals in saltwater lagoons on the northeast coast of South Island. Here the wind nearly always blows, the sun nearly always shines, and rainfall is rare.

THE ECONOMICS OF FARMING

New Zealand is a country with a predominantly one-crop economy—grass. Grass in turn sustains about nine-tenths of her exports. It's a fact often repeated that there are more sheep in New

Zealand than there are people. There are millions more. An approximate count tallies the human population at over three million with the sheep numbering well more than seventy million. It's a simple business of converting grass into meat, cheese, butter, dried milk, and wool. A tremendous amount of research has gone into the process, resulting in increased efficiency.

SCIENCE

New Zealand has universities that offer advanced courses in all subjects. With the agricultural emphasis of its population, it is only natural that much of its efforts are directed toward research in crop and animal development.

Farmland productivity has been achieved by hard work and investment in machinery and fertilizers. Two-thirds of all grassland, which consists of one-third of the whole country, has been improved. Native bush and wiry grass, called tussock, have been plowed under or burned and replaced with imported grasses and clovers.

A big boost to grassland management, especially in the high country, was the introduction in 1949 of sowing seed and fertilizer by airplanes. Today there is a great effort to correct some of the devastation caused by poor management in the past.

MARKETING

New Zealand is finding ways to sell her surplus meat in new markets. Lamb is a popular source of meat in Muslim countries, but there are religious rules that must be followed governing the slaughter of animals. Muslim slaughterers follow the Islamic rules and recite the proscribed prayer over each lamb before it is killed. Also, live sheep are exported to the Middle East.

Packaging meat in various ways has helped sales. Thin slices are sold to Japan, chunks for kabobs go to Greece and the Middle East, while boneless packages are popular in the United States.

New Zealand is still trying to diversify its products for export. Although wool, meat, and cheese are the major exports, other agricultural products have been promoted. The kiwi fruit, at one time only known to tropical climates, is now seen in supermarkets around the world.

Today an area around Golden Bay on the northernmost shoulder of South Island is a rich agricultural area where hops and tobacco are raised, and the nation's largest apple orchards bring in bountiful harvests.

Because so many New Zealanders are engaged in agriculture, there never has been a strong class distinction between town people and those who chose the rural life. In fact, those who owned land outside the cities were often the affluent ones. The result of having so much of the country's wealth dependent on one group of products meant that the economy was prone to fluctuate depending on global markets. However, when the price of meat is down, wool is up.

FORESTS AND FOREST PRODUCTS

To the south of Tokoroa, New Zealanders have been planting trees in one of the largest man-made forests in the world. Over 280,000 acres (113,313 hectares) have been planted.

Present and future generations are reaping the rewards of this

The Tasman Paper Company pulp and paper plant

farsighted project. Sawmills are converting logs into lumber and paper pulp. Everything from writing paper to fiberboard to paper bags is produced. Timber is used for building and for creating wooden packing cases. Currently a much more diverse range of products is being developed, including veneers, plywood, and parquets. A financially profitable trade with Japan has started.

COMMERCIAL FISHING

New Zealand has never really taken full advantage of her commercial fishing territory. She controls by international treaty an exclusive economic zone 199 miles (320 kilometers) from her shores, one of the biggest in the world. Soviet, Japanese, Korean, and Taiwanese fleets also fish in this zone.

TRANSPORTATION AND COMMUNICATION

To explore New Zealand, tourists and natives alike can enjoy a comprehensive and dependable transportation network.

A switchback highway in the Southern Alps (left) and a Mount Cook Airlines plane equipped with skis

Highways connect most of the country's places of scenic, historic, and cultural interest. There are bus lines on both islands that offer brief stops in small towns along their routes.

New Zealand Railways provide passenger rail service between the larger cities and towns. They are equipped with lounge and dining cars. North Island's main line runs between Auckland and Wellington, passing west of Tongariro National Park. Two daily express trains link the two cities. On South Island, train routes branch from Christchurch, south along the coast to Invercargill, west across Arthur's Pass to Greymouth, and north to Picton. A first-class express train links Christchurch, Dunedin, and Invercargill.

Ferries for passengers, cars, and trucks cross Cook Strait several times a day providing service between Wellington at the southern tip of North Island, and Picton, on South Island's Marlborough Sounds. The trip takes about three hours and twenty minutes. Ferry service also links Bluff, at the southern tip of South Island, and Stewart Island.

Air New Zealand, Mount Cook Airlines, and several small

115

Tramping, or hiking, is one way to enjoy New Zealand's spectacular scenery.

regional airlines can take passengers just about anywhere they want to go, but for many New Zealanders the way to go is on foot. Hikers and backpackers scramble over the roughest terrain and some of the most beautiful scenery in the world. New Zealanders call this "tramping."

Efficient telephone service has been an expected part of modern living in the cities, but in the more remote areas of both islands, lines have yet to reach the homes of herders and farmers tucked away in the high country. This is where shortwave radio has come to the rescue.

Television and radio have been providing school broadcasts, news bulletins (including rebroadcasts from the British Broadcasting Corporation in London), sessions with farmers, housewives and children, and coverage of major sporting events, as well as music, lectures, official government announcements, local weather bulletins, and stock-exchange reports. New Zealanders are kept informed.

Lake Tekapo and the Alps in South Canterbury
Inset: A Maori boy in traditional face paint and dress

NEW ZEALAND'S MOST VALUABLE ASSET

With the development of long-range jet travel, tourists are flocking to this country of spectacular scenery that for a long time has been overlooked because of the miles that separated it from any neighbors.

Visitors are beginning to realize that one of its most valuable assets is the friendly attitude of its people. There is a genuine warmth that seems to spread from shore to shore. Whether the visitor is greeted by a Maori in the native tongue or by a pakeha who has learned the words—*haere mai* means "welcome."

MAP KEY

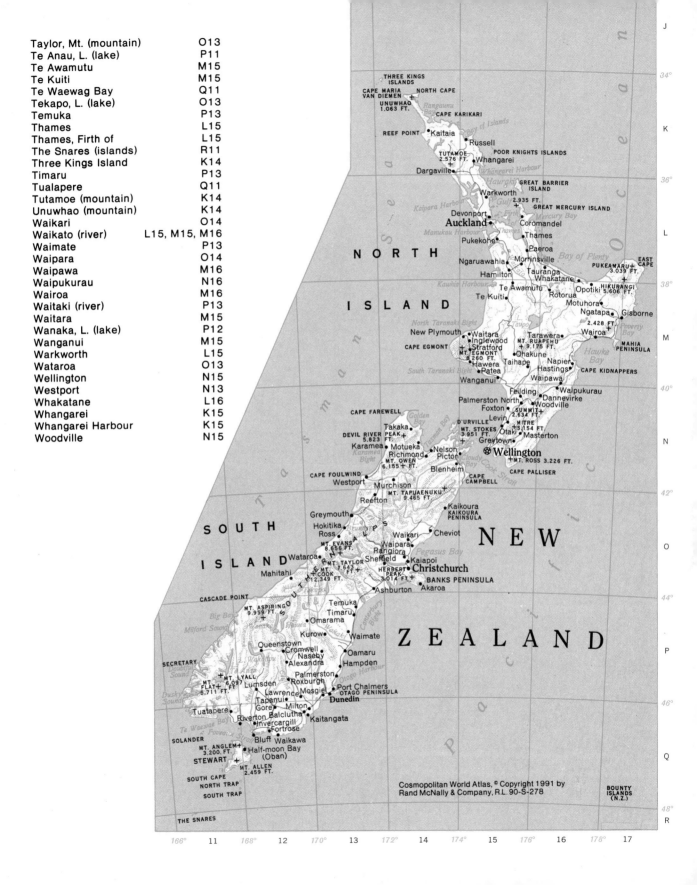

Cosmopolitan World Atlas, © Copyright 1991 by
Rand McNally & Company, R.L. 90-S-278

MINI-FACTS AT A GLANCE

GENERAL INFORMATION

Official Name: New Zealand

Capital: Wellington

Official Language: New Zealand is an English-speaking country. Virtually all Maori speak English, but Maori is taught in a number of schools. The only other non-English language spoken by any significant number of people is Samoan.

Government: New Zealand is an independent sovereign state within the Commonwealth of Nations, with the British monarch as the nominal head of state. Queen Elizabeth II is represented by a governor-general. New Zealand is a constitutional monarchy with a parliamentary form of government based on the British pattern. In 1852 the New Zealand Constitution Act created a Central Legislature, consisting of the governor-general and the General Assembly, which was made up of an appointed Legislative Council and an elected House of Representatives. The Legislative Council was abolished in 1950, and New Zealand now has a unicameral Legislature, elected at least every three years. The government is formed by members of the winning party after an election. New Zealand has had a two-party system with the National or the Labour party in power.

New Zealand law is based on English common law. The administration of justice begins in the local courts. The district judges have only a limited civil and criminal jurisdiction. Appeals go to the high court, and then to the court of appeals, which consists of the chief justice and other senior judges. In addition to these courts there are courts with special functions, such as the Maori land court, family courts, and courts for juvenile offenders.

Anthems: "God Defend New Zealand" (national); "God Save the Queen" (royal)

Flag: The flag has a blue field; at the upper left is a red, white, and blue Union Jack and in the right half of the field are four stars of the Southern Cross in red, bordered by white.

Money: Basic unit—New Zealand dollar (NZ$1). In October 1990 the New Zealand dollar was worth $1.51 in United States currency.

Weights and Measures: The metric system is used.

Population: 3,389,000 (1989 estimate); 84 percent urban, 16 percent rural. About 9 percent of the people are Maori.

Major Cities:

Auckland	820,754
Wellington	325,697

Christchurch 399,373
Manukau. 177,248
Dunedin 106,864
Hamilton. 95,511
(Population based on 1986 census.)

Religion: Anglicans are the largest religious group, followed by Presbyterians and Roman Catholics. There are also a sizable number of Methodists, as well as some minor Protestant sects, some Eastern Orthodox churches, some Jewish congregations, and some Maori adaptations of Christianity. One-fourth of the population does not claim any religious affiliation.

GEOGRAPHY

Highest Point: Mount Cook, 12,349 ft. (3,764 m) above sea level

Lowest Point: Sea level along the coast

Mountains: The Southern Alps form the backbone of the South Island. The main ranges of the North Island, which are only about half as tall as the Southern Alps, stretch northeastward.

Rivers: Many rivers descend from the lakes and glaciers of the Southern Alps. The Rakaia, Rangitata, and Waitaki are the main Canterbury Plains rivers. The Oreti, Mataura, and Waiau are the principal streams to the south. The Clutha is the island's longest river—201 mi. (323 km). The Waikato River is the longest on the North Island—266 mi. (425 km).

Climate: The climate of New Zealand is determined by its latitude and its physical characteristics. There are no extremes of temperature. In most parts of the country, daytime highs in summer are above 70° F. (21° C), occasionally exceeding 81° F. (27° C) in the north. In winter daytime highs throughout the country are rarely below 50° F. (10° C). Rainfall is highest in areas dominated by mountains exposed to the prevailing westerly and northwesterly winds.

Area: 103,883 sq. mi. (269,057 km²)
     North Island—44,244 sq. mi. (114,592 km²)
     South Island—58,965 sq. mi. (152,719 km²)
The North and the South Islands extend in a curve more than 1,000 mi. (1,600 km) long.
     Coastline—About 3,200 mi. (5,150 km)

NATURE

Trees: Mixed evergreen forests cover about two-thirds of the land. The island's isolation has encouraged the development of indigenous species—almost 90 percent of the plants are unknown in the rest of the world. Along the mountain chain running the length of the country, the false beech is the predominant forest tree. European broadleafs are widely used ornamentally, and willows and poplars are frequently planted to prevent erosion on hillsides. The stately kauri tree was prized for building ships and housing by the early settlers.

Animals: Because of New Zealand's isolation there was no higher animal life when the Maori arrived 1,000 or more years ago. There was the gecko, a species of lizard, and the tuatara. In addition to their domestic animals, the English brought other species with them; deer, rabbits, cattle, pigs, and sheep. The red deer and the Australian opossum have multiplied enormously and do untold damage in the high country bush. The control of goats, deer, opossum, and rabbits is an ongoing problem.

Fish: A great variety of fish are found in New Zealand waters. Tuna, marlin, and some big-game sharks are attracted by the warm currents, which are locally populated by snapper, trevally, and kawhwai. Tarakihi, grouper, and bass are found off the entire coastline. Flounder and sole live on tidal mud flats and crayfish live in rocky areas off the coastline.

Birds: New Zealand is a paradise for birds. The flightless kiwi is found in secluded bush areas. The weka and takahe (barely rescued from extinction) probably became flightless after arrival. Some birds, such as the saddleback and the native thrush, are peculiar to New Zealand, but many others, such as the tui, the fantail, and the bellbird, are closely related to Australian birds. Parrots abound in some of the northern areas. The albatross, oystercatcher, and other seabirds also have found their way here.

EVERYDAY LIFE

Food: New Zealanders eat large quantities of meat and dairy products. The favorite meat is lamb. Sweet potatoes are popular. A soup made from clams, called *toheroa*, is regarded as a rare treat. Oysters and whitebait, in season, are popular. Tea is the favorite drink, and beer and wine the favorite alcoholic beverages.

Housing: Most New Zealanders live in single-family homes with enough land for small flower or vegetable gardens. In the larger cities some people live in high-rise apartment buildings. Almost all have refrigerators, washing machines, and other modern conveniences, but few have air conditioning because the weather rarely becomes extremely hot.

Holidays

> January 1 and 2, New Year's Day
> February 6, New Zealand Day, the official name, but usually called Waitangi Day
> Good Friday, the Friday before Easter
> Easter Monday, the Monday after Easter
> April 25, Anzac Day
> First Monday in June, Queen's Birthday
> Fourth Monday in October, Labor Day
> December 25, Christmas Day
> December 26, Boxing Day

Culture: Cultural life in New Zealand is complex. It is predominantly European but also contains elements from many other cultures, particularly the Maori. A renaissance in Maori wood carving, weaving, carved and decorated meetinghouses, songs, and dances has enriched the cultural climate. Maori art is displayed in many galleries and museums.

New Zealand's Katherine Mansfield is considered one of the finest writers of short stories in English. Among her successors was Frank Sargeson who began publishing stories in the 1930s and also published a long series of novels and autobiographies. Novelists such as Janet Frame and Sylvia Ashton-Warner have received international acclaim.

The great expansion of painting came after World War II, and numerous galleries opened to exhibit the work of a "vigorous art scene." Painter Frances Hodgkins is internationally known.

Professional theater companies have developed in the larger cities.

Organized music began with choral societies in the mid-nineteenth century. The New Zealand Symphony Orchestra occasionally has given concerts abroad. Opera star Kiri te Kanawa is famous throughout the world.

Sports and Recreation: Sports are the main leisure-time activity of most of the population. There is widespread participation in rugby football and cricket. Horse racing is a popular spectator sport.

New Zealand was founded by people who braved the sea in primitive canoes, and that tradition has been kept alive by using the water for sport and recreation. In the 1988 America's Cup classic the beautiful *New Zealand* was a worthy competitor. New Zealand teams have won many championship rowing contests and have collected Olympic gold medals in that sport. World-class white water kayakers, canoeists, and rafters have trained in New Zealand's ocean paradise.

Mountaineering produced the first man to climb Mt. Everest—Sir Edmund Hillary.

Communication: Newspapers carry a high standard of reporting, with substantial coverage of world news provided by foreign agencies. No daily paper has a national circulation, but some from the larger cities are distributed widely.

Almost every family owns at least one television set and one or more radios. The telephone and telegraph systems are privately owned. In some remote areas shortwave radios take the place of telephones.

Transportation: Almost all New Zealanders have an automobile, and the highway system is excellent. Ferries cross Cook Strait several times a day and carry automobiles between the North and South Islands. The government operates a railway system that links the major cities. Air New Zealand and Ansett New Zealand provide international and domestic service. There are international connections at Auckland, Christchurch, and Wellington.

Schools: Education is free, secular, and compulsory between the ages of 6 and 15. The state also subsidizes preschools. There are more than 100 private primary and secondary schools, most of them run by religious groups. Technical institutes, community colleges, and teachers' colleges form the basis of higher education. There are also seven universities. There is a correspondence school for children in remote areas, and continuing education and adult-education centers provide opportunities for lifelong learning.

Health and Welfare: New Zealand has one of the oldest social security systems in the world. Noncontributory old-age pensions were introduced in 1898. Pensions for widows and minors followed soon after, and child allowances were introduced in the 1920s. In 1938 the most extensive system of pensions and welfare in the world was introduced; it provided free hospital treatment, free pharmaceutical service, and heavily subsidized treatment by physicians.

ECONOMY AND INDUSTRY

Principal Products:
Agriculture: Cattle, sheep, deer, apples, kiwi fruit, barley, onions, potatoes, wheat, milk, wool, butter, cheese, meat, wine, and grapes
Fishing: tuna, snapper, cod, flounder
Forestry: radiata pine and Douglas fir are grown on plantations
Manufacturing: Chemicals, iron and steel, paper, wood products, textiles, beef, lamb, and mutton, butter, cheese, dried milk products, machinery, motor vehicles

IMPORTANT DATES

c. A.D. 800 — Possible arrival of the Maori

1642 — Abel Janszoon Tasman becomes the first European to sight New Zealand from his ship

1769 — Captain James Cook explores the main islands

early 1800s — Beginning of British colonization

1814 — Samuel Marsden starts a missionary post

1820 — First plough is brought to New Zealand

1820s-40s — "Musket Wars" among New Zealand tribes

1830s — European speculators try to gain ownership of New Zealand's land

1834 — William Colenso arrives with a printing press, which is used to print the Bible in the Maori language

1835 — Charles Darwin visits New Zealand

1840 — The Maori chiefs sign the Treaty of Waitangi, giving Great Britain sovereignty over New Zealand

1841 — William Hobson becomes the first governor-general of New Zealand

1845-70 — New Zealand Wars, fighting between settlers and the Maori on North Island

1852 — New Zealand is given a constitution

1856 — William Thompson, son of Chief Waharoa, begins to unite the Waikato people in the "King Movement"; export wheat market fails

1858 — "King Movement" results in selection of Te Wherowhero as a single chief to unite the tribes

1861—Gold rush begins

1863—European troops invade the Waikato stronghold of the King Movement

1865—New Zealand is granted the right to form its own government

1867—The Maori gain the right to elect four representatives to Parliament

1868-72—Te Kooti's War (the last two years Te Kooti was on the run)

1882—The *Dunedin*, a refrigerated ship, transports fresh meat from New Zealand to England, opening up a new industry

1893—New Zealand becomes the first nation to grant women the right to vote

1907—New Zealand becomes a dominion within the British Empire

1914-18—New Zealand joins the Allies in the fight against Germany in World War I

1918—Influenza epidemic kills many Maori

1930s—Great Depression causes prices to fall and unemployment is widespread

1935-38—Full-scale social security and comprehensive health care systems are enacted

1939-45—New Zealand fights with the Allies against Germany, Italy, and Japan in World War II

1962—An ombudsman position is created in Parliament

1967—Basic unit of money becomes the NZ dollar

1985—Nuclear weapons and nuclear-powered ships are banned from New Zealand's ports

IMPORTANT PEOPLE

Thomas Burns (1796-1871), Cofounder of Dunedin (with William Cargill); nephew of poet Robert Burns

William Cargill (1784-1860), Scots man who settled Invercargill and Dunedin and established a Free Church of Scotland

William Colenso (1811-1899), arrived in New Zealand in 1834 with the first printing press; printed Bibles and prayer books in the Maori language

Captain James Cook (1728-79), English mariner and explorer, charted coasts of New Zealand, Australia, and New Guinea

Bob Fitzsimmons (1862-1917), boxer

Murray Halberg (1933-   ), runner

Sir Edmund Hillary (1919-   ), explorer and mountain climber, first to climb Mt. Everest

William Hobson (1792-1842), British naval captain who signed the Treaty of Waitangi on February 6, 1840; New Zealand's first governor

Frances Hodgkins (1869-1947), painter

Keith Holyoake (1904-84), prime minister, came to power with Nationalist victory of 1949

Dennis Hulme (1936-   ), racing car driver

Thomas Kendall (1778-1832), compiled the first short dictionary of the Maori language

Norman Kirk (1923-74), prime minister, came to power with Labour party victory of 1972

David Lange (1942-   ), Labour party prime minister, affirmed his party's pledge in 1986 to ban all vessels carrying nuclear weapons or powered by nuclear energy from New Zealand ports

Katherine Mansfield (1888-1923), author

Samuel Marsden (1765-1838), arrived in New Zealand in 1814 to set up missionary post under auspices of Anglican Church Missionary Society

Sir Apirana Ngata (1874-1950), Maori leader who served in Parliament; helped preserve Maori traditions, compiled *Ngo Moteatea*, an anthology of Maori tribal songs and chants

Gabriel Read (1824?-94), prospector from California who found gold on the South Island in 1861

Peter Snell (1938-   ), runner; Olympic gold medal winner

Abel Janszoon Tasman (1603-59), Dutch sea captain who was the first to spot New Zealand, in 1642

Kiri te Kanawa (1944-   ), opera star

Te Kooti (c.1830-93), Maori leader who massacred white settlers (1868-72), as warning to others to stay out of their territory

King Te Wherowhero (?-1860), Maori who ruled the King Country for several years

Anthony Wilding (1883-1915), tennis star

INDEX

Page numbers that appear in boldface type indicate illustrations

126

About the Author

Mary Virginia Fox was graduated from Northwestern University and now lives near Madison, Wisconsin, conveniently located across the lake from the state capital and the University of Wisconsin. She is the author of more than two dozen books for young people and a score of feature articles for adult publications. In the Enchantment of the World series, she also has written *Tunisia, Iran,* and *Gabon.*

She and her husband are world travelers. She feels New Zealand is a country to be enjoyed by those interested in geology, anthropology, the history of world exploration, and surely the arts.